Truffle Quick Start Guide

Learn the fundamentals of Ethereum development

Nikhil Bhaskar

BIRMINGHAM - MUMBAI

Truffle Quick Start Guide

Copyright © 2018 Packt Publishing

All rights reserved. No part of this book may be reproduced, stored in a retrieval system, or transmitted in any form or by any means, without the prior written permission of the publisher, except in the case of brief quotations embedded in critical articles or reviews.

Every effort has been made in the preparation of this book to ensure the accuracy of the information presented. However, the information contained in this book is sold without warranty, either express or implied. Neither the author(s), nor Packt Publishing or its dealers and distributors, will be held liable for any damages caused or alleged to have been caused directly or indirectly by this book.

Packt Publishing has endeavored to provide trademark information about all of the companies and products mentioned in this book by the appropriate use of capitals. However, Packt Publishing cannot guarantee the accuracy of this information.

Commissioning Editor: Kunal Chaudhari
Acquisition Editor: Reshma Raman
Content Development Editor: Mohammed Yusuf Imaratwale
Technical Editor: Sushmeeta Jena
Copy Editor: Safis Editing
Project Coordinator: Hardik Bhinde
Proofreader: Safis Editing
Indexer: Tejal Daruwale Soni
Graphics: Jason Monteiro
Production Coordinator: Deepika Naik

First published: June 2018

Production reference: 1260618

Published by Packt Publishing Ltd.
Livery Place
35 Livery Street
Birmingham
B3 2PB, UK.

ISBN 978-1-78913-254-0

www.packtpub.com

mapt.io

Mapt is an online digital library that gives you full access to over 5,000 books and videos, as well as industry leading tools to help you plan your personal development and advance your career. For more information, please visit our website.

Why subscribe?

- Spend less time learning and more time coding with practical eBooks and Videos from over 4,000 industry professionals
- Improve your learning with Skill Plans built especially for you
- Get a free eBook or video every month
- Mapt is fully searchable
- Copy and paste, print, and bookmark content

PacktPub.com

Did you know that Packt offers eBook versions of every book published, with PDF and ePub files available? You can upgrade to the eBook version at www.PacktPub.com and as a print book customer, you are entitled to a discount on the eBook copy. Get in touch with us at service@packtpub.com for more details.

At www.PacktPub.com, you can also read a collection of free technical articles, sign up for a range of free newsletters, and receive exclusive discounts and offers on Packt books and eBooks.

Contributors

About the author

Nikhil Bhaskar is the founder and CEO of Ulixir Inc—a newly founded tech company that builds decentralized and traditional software.

He completed B9lab's Ethereum Developer Course, and he is now a certified Ethereum developer.

Aside from running Ulixir, he spends his time traveling and eating. He is a bit of a digital nomad; this year, he's lived in five countries and plans to live in six more before the year ends.

About the reviewer

Aasim is a full-stack blockchain engineer at Inncretech LLC, Princeton, New Jersey. He has a masters degree in Information Systems with a graduate certification in Business Intelligence from Steven's Institute Of Technology, Hoboken, New Jersey. He works with the R&D team of blockchain and data science for making POCs around AI, Ethereum and Hyperledger blockchain for clients to incorporate in their proprietary systems, which helps them upgrade to new cutting-edge technologies.

> *I would like to thank my family and friends for supporting me on my journey of life, which helped me grow into a knowledgeable and intellectual person. I would also like to express my gratitude to my company's co-founder and CTO for believing in me and giving me this opportunity to explore blockchain in depth. I would sincerely like to thank the author and his team for giving me this opportunity to review this book.*

Packt is searching for authors like you

If you're interested in becoming an author for Packt, please visit `authors.packtpub.com` and apply today. We have worked with thousands of developers and tech professionals, just like you, to help them share their insight with the global tech community. You can make a general application, apply for a specific hot topic that we are recruiting an author for, or submit your own idea.

Preface

This book provides an intuitive, step-by-step, and engaging guide on how to write smart contracts and build decentralized applications with Truffle on Ethereum blockchains.

The first section will cover the basics of Truffle, briefly explain how it integrates Solidity and Web3, and get the reader to build a mini-decentralized application. The following sections will dive into migration, testing, and combining Truffle with popular JavaScript frameworks. The final section of this book will cover the best practices and common mistakes in Truffle to increase the reader's level of proficiency in building Dapps with Truffle.

This book will contain code snippets, exercises, and a project that the reader will continuously build throughout their reading journey.

Who this book is for

This book is for JavaScript developers who are interested in learning about writing smart contracts and building decentralized applications on blockchain. The reader of this book will be required to have some basic understanding of JavaScript and web services. Basic knowledge of Ethereum and/or blockchain is also required.

What this book covers

Chapter 1, *Truffle for Decentralized Applications*, introduces you to Truffle and explains why it is used and how it works from a high level. It will also demonstrate how JavaScript, Solidity, and Web3 interact inside the basic Truffle environment.

Chapter 2, *Web3 and Solidity in Truffle,* concerns Web3 and its related APIs and uses in Truffle. You will gain an understanding of the fundamentals of Web3 and how it is used in Truffle.

Chapter 3, *Choosing an Ethereum Client for Your Dapp*, is about various Ethereum clients, and will highlight the use case for each one and show you how to integrate each Ethereum client with your Truffle application.

Preface

Chapter 4, *Migrating Your Dapp to Ethereum Blockchains*, teaches you how to correctly migrate your Truffle application to Ethereum blockchains. You will also learn about common pitfalls when attempting to migrate your application.

Chapter 5, *Truffle and Popular JavaScript Technologies*, illustrates the use of Truffle with modern JavaScript technologies such as Angular, React, and Node.js. You will learn how to integrate Truffle with JavaScript frontend libraries and frameworks as well as on the backend with Node.js.

Chapter 6, *Testing Your Dapp*, demonstrates to you the importance of thoroughly testing your smart contracts, detailing various techniques and approaches for successfully testing a Truffle application.

Chapter 7, *Truffle Gotchas and Best Practices*, explains the common mistakes people make when developing with Truffle, as well as how to remedy them. Lastly, you will learn and understand how to diagnose and resolve common blockchain issues, such as chain syncing, as well as some best security practices.

To get the most out of this book

As mentioned before, basic knowledge of JavaScript and web development, as well as of Ethereum/blockchain, is required. To get the most out of this book, have the GitHub repository (mentioned in the chapters) by your side; simply follow the instructions outlined in each chapter.

Download the example code files

You can download the example code files for this book from your account at `www.packtpub.com`. If you purchased this book elsewhere, you can visit `www.packtpub.com/support` and register to have the files emailed directly to you.

You can download the code files by following these steps:

1. Log in or register at `www.packtpub.com`.
2. Select the **SUPPORT** tab.
3. Click on **Code Downloads & Errata**.
4. Enter the name of the book in the **Search** box and follow the onscreen instructions.

Once the file is downloaded, please make sure that you unzip or extract the folder using the latest version of:

- WinRAR/7-Zip for Windows
- Zipeg/iZip/UnRarX for Mac
- 7-Zip/PeaZip for Linux

The code bundle for the book is also hosted on GitHub at https://github.com/PacktPublishing/Truffle-Quick-Start-Guide. In case there's an update to the code, it will be updated on the existing GitHub repository.

We also have other code bundles from our rich catalog of books and videos available at https://github.com/PacktPublishing/. Check them out!

Download the color images

We also provide a PDF file that has color images of the screenshots/diagrams used in this book. You can download it here: http://www.packtpub.com/sites/default/files/downloads/TruffleQuickStartGuide_ColorImages.pdf.

Code in Action

Visit the following link to check out videos of the code being run: http://bit.ly/2K80ovD

Conventions used

There are a number of text conventions used throughout this book.

`CodeInText`: Indicates code words in text, database table names, folder names, filenames, file extensions, pathnames, dummy URLs, user input, and Twitter handles. Here is an example: "Mount the downloaded `WebStorm-10*.dmg` disk image file as another disk in your system."

Preface

A block of code is set as follows:

```
web3.eth.getAccounts(callback(error, result){ ... })
```

When we wish to draw your attention to a particular part of a code block, the relevant lines or items are set in bold:

```
web3.eth.getAccounts()
  .then(function (accounts) {
    console.log(JSON.stringify(accounts, null, 2));
  })
  .catch(function (error) {
    console.error(error);
  });
```

Any command-line input or output is written as follows:

```
make geth
```

Bold: Indicates a new term, an important word, or words that you see onscreen. For example, words in menus or dialog boxes appear in the text like this. Here is an example: "Select **System info** from the **Administration** panel."

Warnings or important notes appear like this.

Tips and tricks appear like this.

Get in touch

Feedback from our readers is always welcome.

General feedback: Email `feedback@packtpub.com` and mention the book title in the subject of your message. If you have questions about any aspect of this book, please email us at `questions@packtpub.com`.

Errata: Although we have taken every care to ensure the accuracy of our content, mistakes do happen. If you have found a mistake in this book, we would be grateful if you would report this to us. Please visit www.packtpub.com/submit-errata, selecting your book, clicking on the Errata Submission Form link, and entering the details.

Piracy: If you come across any illegal copies of our works in any form on the Internet, we would be grateful if you would provide us with the location address or website name. Please contact us at copyright@packtpub.com with a link to the material.

If you are interested in becoming an author: If there is a topic that you have expertise in and you are interested in either writing or contributing to a book, please visit authors.packtpub.com.

Reviews

Please leave a review. Once you have read and used this book, why not leave a review on the site that you purchased it from? Potential readers can then see and use your unbiased opinion to make purchase decisions, we at Packt can understand what you think about our products, and our authors can see your feedback on their book. Thank you!

For more information about Packt, please visit packtpub.com.

Truffle for Decentralized Applications

This chapter will introduce you to Truffle, and explain why it is used and how it works from a high level. Moreover, this chapter will demonstrate how JavaScript, Solidity, and web3 interact inside the basic Truffle environment, and how Truffle gives the developer control over all three said aspects of a decentralized application. Lastly, you will build a small project in Truffle and understand its power.

Specifically, you will:

- Learn and understand the reasons for the use of Truffle
- Learn and understand how Truffle harnesses popular technologies, such as JavaScript and web3, from a high level
- Learn and understand how to write basic decentralized applications in Truffle

Technical requirements

You will be required to have basic knowledge of JavaScript and web development as well as Ethereum/blockchain. Finally, to use the Git repository of this book, the user needs to install Git.

The code files of this chapter can be found on GitHub:
`https://github.com/PacktPublishing/Truffle-Quick-Start-Guide/tree/master/Chapter01`

Check out the following video to see the code in action:
`http://bit.ly/2MfQSnk`

What is Truffle?

In short, Truffle is a framework to write, compile, deploy, and test decentralized applications on Ethereum blockchains. For this chapter, you can also think of Truffle as a framework that attempts to seamlessly integrate smart contract development and traditional web development.

Granularly, within the Truffle environment, you can write JavaScript for the frontend, Solidity for smart contracts, and use web3 as a bridge to connect various blockchain networks to the client.

If you are not familiar with web3, or you need a refresher on Solidity, worry not. The subsequent chapter will cover these two technologies in sufficient detail before you start building more complex decentralized applications.

For now, it is enough to know that Truffle combines JavaScript, Solidity, and web3 to allow you to write complete and testable decentralized applications:

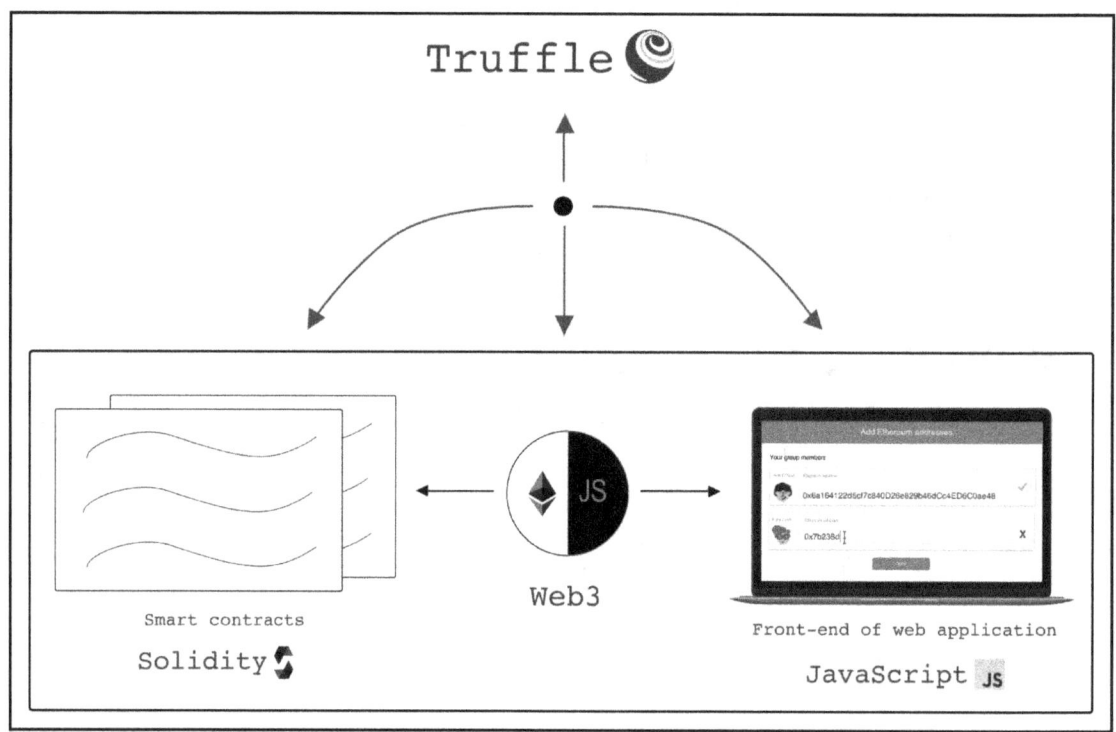

Can you write decentralized applications without Truffle? Sure you can. Truffle simply makes the process of compiling, building, and migrating your application easier by automating certain monotonous aspects.

You will see how this is done toward the end of this chapter when you build a small but complete decentralized application. I will walk you through code snippets, provide a working repository for reference, and explain to you fundamental build concepts as you write code. Most importantly, I want to ensure you start coding as soon as possible. So, let's get started.

Let's build a mini Dapp

The best way to start is with a simple *Hello World* app, but we can do better than that. Let's build a simple *Dapp* that you will have the chance to expand upon throughout this entire book. This way, you can build a *Dapp* like a true software engineer; that is, you will iteratively add features and make improvements to your application as you see fit.

Let's build a to-do list

Productivity is a virtue that resonates a lot with software engineers and developers alike. In the book *Algorithms to Live By*, Brian Christian states that:

> "When the future is foggy, it turns out you don't need a calendar—just a to-do list."

Many of us have come to know that a to-do list helps to organize chaos.

So, let's create a to-do list, except with a little twist. This will be a to-do list on the blockchain, where you get others to do your work for you. Of course, you have to pay them with a token, call it TodoCoin, for their work.

You will create this app as the *owner* of the contract, and the individuals performing your tasks will be referred to as *doers*.

As an owner, you must be able to:

- Create a task with a title, description, and TodoCoin reward amount
- Accept a completed task
- Reject a completed task
- Reward a doer for successful review of a completed task

As a doer, you must be able to:

1. Start a task
2. Finish a task
3. Withdraw owed rewards for successful reviews of completed tasks

If this seems like a handful, worry not. You will not build all specifications of this *Dapp* in this chapter. For this chapter, as promised, you will build a simplified version of this *Dapp*. Later, see if you can slowly start building the other specifications on your own.

For this chapter, you will simply do the following:

- Allow an owner to create the contract
- Allow an owner to transfer a TodoCoin reward to a specified address

That's it. You will assume three things:

- The task has been successfully completed and reviewed off-chain
- The recipient of the reward is a valid doer
- The reward amount is the correct amount for the task

Also, a decentralized application is not complete without a decent user interface. So, you will build a simple interface that allows the owner of a contract to enter a TodoCoin reward amount and transfer it to an address of their choice.

The final version will look like this:

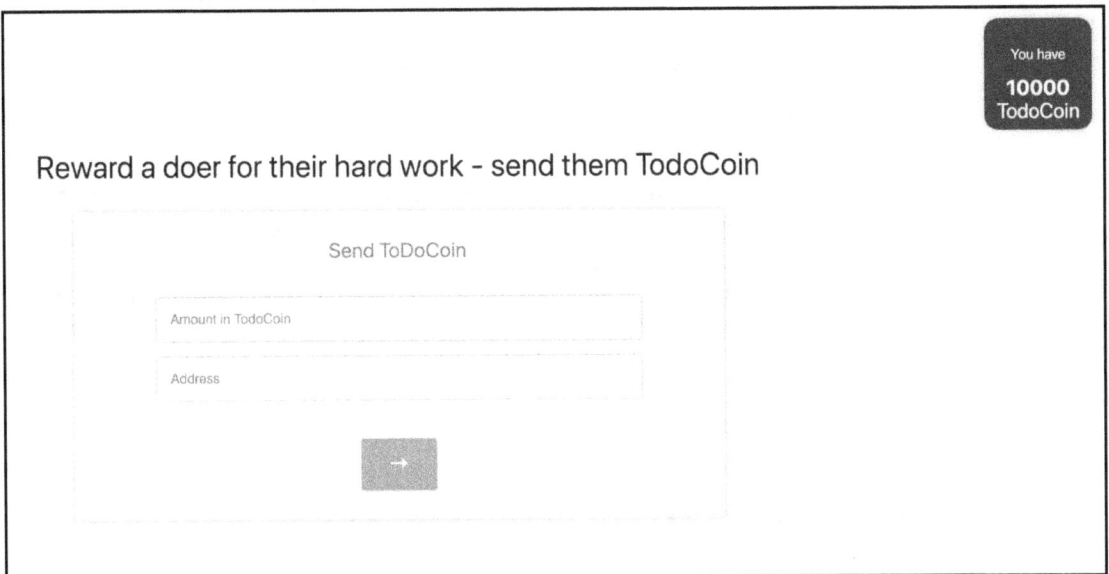

What frameworks will we be using?

The only framework you will use for this chapter is Truffle, actually. This way, you can focus purely on the Truffle elements of this mini *Dapp* without getting muddled in implementation details of other frameworks. But don't worry, in later chapters, you will learn how to integrate Truffle with Angular, React, and Node.

Initializing a Truffle project

First things first. Head over to Google. Then, perform the following:

- **Search for** `truffle webpack`.
- The first result should be a Github link (`https://github.com/trufflesuite/truffle-init-webpack`). Click it.

- Follow the installation steps. In other words, perform the following:
    1. Open a terminal window, and install Truffle globally with `npm install -g truffle`.
    2. Create a new folder called `truffle-practice`.
    3. Inside `truffle-practice` create another folder called `chapter1`.
    4. Go into the `chapter1` folder.
    5. Download the truffle Webpack box. This also takes care of installing the necessary dependencies: `truffle unbox webpack`.

The structure inside of the `truffle-practice` folder should look like this—the important folders and files are in **bold**:

```
└── chapter1
    ├── app
    │   ├── index.html
    │   ├── ; javascripts
    │   │   └── app.js
    │   └── stylesheets
    │       └── app.css
    ├── contracts
    │   ├── ConvertLib.sol
    │   ├── MetaCoin.sol
    │   └── Migrations.sol
    ├── migrations
    │   ├── 1_initial_migration.js
    │   └── 2_deploy_contracts.js
    ├── package-lock.json
    ├── package.json
    ├── test
    │   ├── TestMetacoin.sol
    │   └── metacoin.js
    ├── truffle.js
    └── webpack.config.js
```

Your structure may look a little different depending on the time you ran the preceding steps, but the folders of concern are `/app`, `/contracts`, `/migrations`, and `/test`. The root files of concern are `package.json` and `truffle.js`.

Peeping into the folders

Here are the important folders:

- `app`: This folder contains the JavaScript, HTML, and CSS files of your decentralized application. Notice how we have a folder for `/javascripts` and `/stylesheets`, and a root `index.html` file.

- `contracts`: This folder contains the smart contracts for your decentralized application. Notice the Solidity files `ConvertLib.sol`, `MetaCoin.sol`, and `Migrations.sol`.

- `migrations`: This folder contains the scripts to migrate and deploy our smart contracts properly to various Ethereum blockchains. You will see this in more detail in `Chapter 4`, *Migrating Your Dapp to Ethereum Blockchains*.

- `tests`: This folder contains the files with unit and integration tests. You will see this in more detail in `Chapter 6`, *Testing Your Dapp*.

Peeping into the root files

Here are the important root files:

- `package.json`: This is a standard file that includes all the production and development dependencies of our project. Have a look through the dependencies if you are interested.

- `truffle.js`: This file contains configuration details about migrating your smart contracts to a specific Ethereum network. For now, you will simply connect to a local network. You will learn how to migrate your smart contract to various Ethereum networks in `Chapter 4`, *Migrating Your Dapp to Ethereum Blockchains*.

Here's a quick snippet:

```
// Allows us to use ES6 in our migrations and tests.
require('babel-register')

module.exports = {
  networks: {
    development: {
      host: '127.0.0.1',
      port: 7545,
```

```
        network_id: '*' // Match any network id
    }
  }
}
```

Housekeeping before we write code

We need to delete a few files and folders first. This is because we won't be working with the default Solidity, JavaScript, and HTML files that come with the Truffle starter project. We will be building everything from scratch, so we need to get rid of a few things; that way, you can see how everything works from the ground up.

Delete a few unnecessary files:

- `contracts/MetaCoin.sol`
- `contracts/ConvertLib.sol`

Delete all the contents inside the following files, but **do not** delete the actual files:

- `app/javascripts/app.js`
- `app/stylesheets/app.css`
- `app/index.html`

Writing our first smart contract

To start writing our first smart contract, we must do the following:

1. Head over to `https://github.com/PacktPublishing/Truffle-Quick-Start-Guide` and clone it. That's where the fully working projects for each chapter are. You can `git clone` the entire repository to keep as a reference when working through this chapter.
2. To ensure we follow proper formatting and camel-case naming conventions, replace `Migrations.sol` with the contents of `https://github.com/PacktPublishing/Truffle-Quick-Start-Guide/blob/master/chapter1/contracts/Migrations.sol`.
    - Unfortunately, the original `Migrations.sol` file is poorly formatted and uses snake-case variable naming, so this step is necessary

3. Create a new file under /contracts, called TaskMaster.sol.
   - This is where your logic for instantiating your to-do list contract and rewarding a doer will live.

Start by creating the constructor, and define an array to hold the current TodoCoin balances of everyone in the contract:

```
pragma solidity ^0.4.17;

contract TaskMaster {
    mapping (address => uint) public balances; // balances of everyone

    function TaskMaster() public {
        balances[msg.sender] = 10000;
    }
}
```

Notice how we hardcode a value of 10000 to the initiator of this contract. Let's go with this for now. We can think of this to mean that the initiator of the TaskMaster contract starts off with a balance of 10000 TodoCoins.

Adding an owner

It's a good idea to have an owner of a contract and give them the sole right to perform admin-level actions such as the rewarding of a doer, so let's define and set an owner:

```
pragma solidity ^0.4.17;

contract TaskMaster {
    mapping (address => uint) public balances; // balances of everyone
    address public owner; // owner of the contract

    function TaskMaster() public {
        owner = msg.sender;
        balances[msg.sender] = 10000;
    }
}
```

The owner of the contract is set to msg.sender, the address instantiating the contract. You will learn more about msg.sender and other Solidity special variables in the next chapter.

Creating a reward method

This will be invoked by the owner to reward a doer for their successful completion of a task:

```
pragma solidity ^0.4.17;

contract TaskMaster {
    mapping (address => uint) public balances; // balances of everyone
    address public owner; // owner of the contract

    function TaskMaster() public {
        owner = msg.sender;
        balances[msg.sender] = 10000;
    }

    function reward(address doer, uint rewardAmount)
        public
        returns(bool sufficientFunds)
    {
        balances[msg.sender] -= rewardAmount;
        balances[doer] += rewardAmount;
        return sufficientFunds;
    }
}
```

This function accepts the following:

- an address for the doer
- an integer amount for their reward

We are almost there—we need to add some necessary security touches.

Notice how we are not performing a real transfer of ETH, but rather we simply decrement the balance of the owner and increment the balance of the doer. The reason we don't perform a real transfer here is because we simply hard-coded a balance value of 10000 and made up a token called TodoCoin. Remember, our goal in this chapter is to get a fully functioning *Dapp* using Truffle.

Securing your contract with modifiers

To ensure that our contract is secure, we ensure the following:

- Only an owner can call the `reward` function
- The owner of the contract has sufficient funds to transfer to the doer

Let's add a few modifiers, `isOwner` and `hasSufficientFunds`:

```
pragma solidity ^0.4.17;

contract TaskMaster {
    mapping (address => uint) public balances; // balances of everyone
    address public owner; // owner of the contract

    function TaskMaster() public {
        owner = msg.sender;
        balances[msg.sender] = 10000;
    }

    function reward(address doer, uint rewardAmount)
        public
        isOwner()
        hasSufficientFunds(rewardAmount)
        returns(bool sufficientFunds)
    {
        balances[msg.sender] -= rewardAmount;
        balances[doer] += rewardAmount;
        return sufficientFunds;
    }

    modifier isOwner() {
        require(msg.sender == owner);
        _;
    }

    modifier hasSufficientFunds(uint rewardAmount) {
        require(balances[msg.sender] >= rewardAmount);
        _;
    }
}
```

`isOwner` requires that the sender of the `reward` function is the owner of the contract. `hasSufficientFunds` requires that the sender of the contract has enough funds to reward the doer.

Adding a utility method

Utility methods help us get data from our contract without modifying the state.

```
function getBalance(address addr) public view returns(uint) {
    return balances[addr];
}
```

This function accepts an address and returns the balance of the passed-in address. Notice how it is marked with `view`. The `view` modifier signifies that this function does not modify the storage state of the contract. You will learn more about this in Chapter 2, *Web3 and Solidity in Truffle*, where we will refresh Solidity fundamentals.

Wrapping up

Your final `TaskMaster.sol` file should look like this:

```
pragma solidity ^0.4.17;

contract TaskMaster {
    mapping (address => uint) public balances; // balances of everyone
    address public owner; // owner of the contract

    function TaskMaster() public {
        owner = msg.sender;
        balances[msg.sender] = 10000;
    }

    function reward(address doer, uint rewardAmount)
        public
        isOwner()
        hasSufficientFunds(rewardAmount)
        returns(bool sufficientFunds)
    {
        balances[msg.sender] -= rewardAmount;
        balances[doer] += rewardAmount;
        return sufficientFunds;
    }
```

```
    function getBalance(address addr) public view returns(uint) {
        return balances[addr];
    }

    modifier isOwner() {
        require(msg.sender == owner);
        _;
    }

    modifier hasSufficientFunds(uint rewardAmount) {
        require(balances[msg.sender] >= rewardAmount);
        _;
    }
}
```

You can also find this file in the repo, under contracts (https://github.com/PacktPublishing/Truffle-Quick-Start-Guide/blob/master/chapter1/contracts/TaskMaster.sol).

Now that we've created a full `TaskMaster.sol` file, you can do the following bit of housekeeping.

Delete all contents of `migrations/2_deploy_contracts.js` and replace them with the following code:

```
var TaskMaster = artifacts.require("./TaskMaster.sol");

module.exports = function(deployer) {
  deployer.deploy(TaskMaster);
};
```

This specifies that `TaskMaster.sol` should be deployed to a blockchain. You will learn more about migrations in Chapter 4, *Migrating Your Dapp to Ethereum Blockchains*.

Building a user interface

Let's create a quick and easy UI for this. It will allow the owner to specify a reward amount and the doer's addresses. It will also display the owner's balance in TodoCoin at all times.

Here's what your final UI will look like:

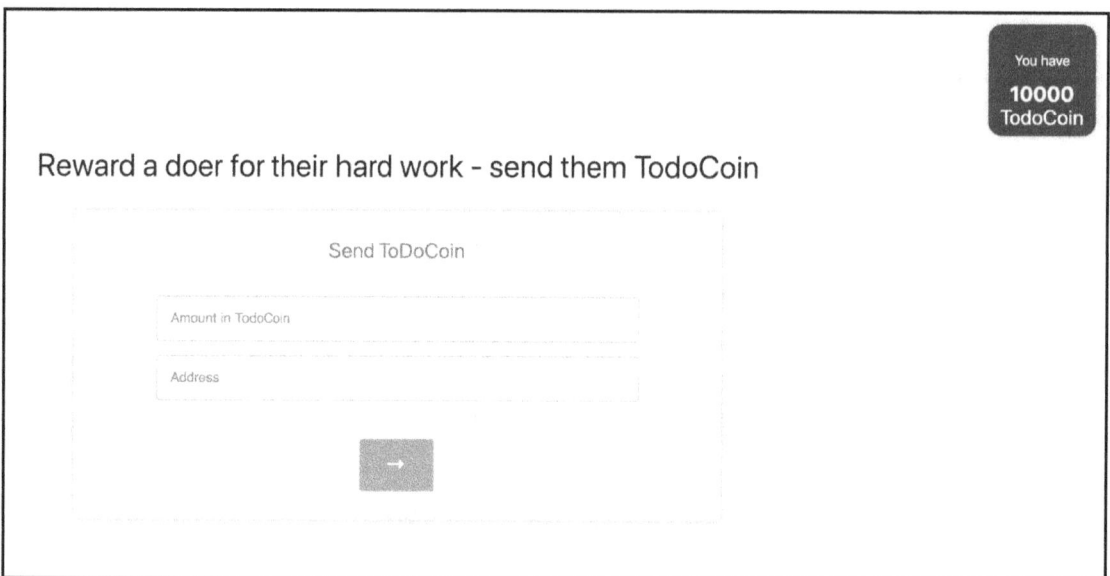

Simple styling

To style, we will use the Tachyons CSS library. It is a utility library that allows you to style your app while writing as little CSS as possible. You can view all the styles here at http://tachyons.io/docs/table-of-styles/.

Performing the build steps

To see our *Dapp* in action, we need to perform the following build steps. Follow them precisely to ensure we get a clean build every time. Essentially, we are compiling and migrating our contracts, then serving our web content.

1. `cd chapter1`.
2. `truffle develop`.
3. Inside the Truffle development console, run the following:
    1. `compile` (this compiles our contracts)
    2. `migrate` (this migrates our contract to the network specified in `truffle.js`)

4. In another terminal window/tab, in the `chapter1` folder, run `npm run dev`.
5. Navigate to `http://localhost:8080/#/`.

 Depending on the version of `truffle` you install, you may see warnings thrown in your console after you compile your contracts. For example, at the time of the writing of this book, constructors share the same name as the contract (that is `TaskMaster`). But in newer versions of truffle, it is preferred to use the `constructor(...) { ... }` syntax instead. Since these are warnings, you can choose to adjust your code based on the warning, or not, and simply continue.

The following steps you just performed are the necessary build steps. I will now refer to them as **Build Steps**, because you will be doing this often throughout this book.

Once you run the **Build Steps**, you will notice a blank screen. That's because `app/index.html` is empty. Let's add some content:

```
<!DOCTYPE html>
<html>
<head>
  <title>Truffle - Mini Dapp</title>
  <link rel="stylesheet"
    href="https://unpkg.com/tachyons@4.9.1/css/tachyons.min.css"/>
  <script src="./app.js"></script>
</head>
<body class="sans-serif pa4">
</body>
</html>
```

We created a `title` in our HTML page called `Truffle - Mini Dapp`, and we added a few CSS references:

- A CDN to the Tachyons library
- A reference to the currently empty `app.js`
- A `body` tag with a *sans-serif* font and padding on all sides

Now, let's add the form. Add the following piece of code inside the body tag:

```
<div class="tc f2 mt6 near-black">Reward a doer for their hard work - send them TodoCoin</div>
 <div class="pa4 mt4 bg-white shadow-1 br2 tc mw7 center">
    <div class="f3 dark-green">Send TodoCoin</div>
    <form class="pt3 pb4 ph5-l black-60">
      <fieldset class="ba b--transparent ph0 mh0">
```

```
            <div class="mt3 ph3 pa0-l">
              <input
                class="pa3 input-reset ba b--black-30 br2 bg-white-smoke w-
                    100"
                type="number"
                id="todoCoinReward"
                placeholder="Amount in TodoCoin">
            </div>
            <div class="mt3 ph3 pa0-l">
              <input
                class="pa3 input-reset ba b--black-30 br2 bg-white-smoke w-
                    100"
                type="text"
                id="doer"
                placeholder="Address">
            </div>
          </fieldset>
      </form>
      <button
        class="white pa3 ph4 bg-green br2 f3 b pointer">→
      </button>
</div>
```

Your screen should now look like this:

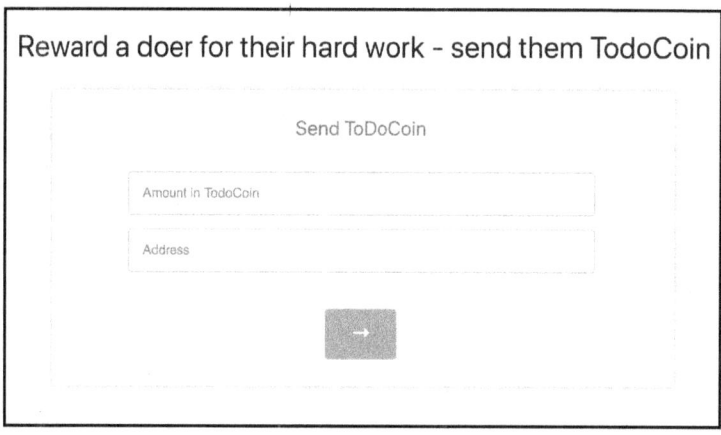

Take a few minutes to look through the HTML and CSS content and understand how this form is being rendered. It's just CSS and HTML, and the classes are all Tachyons classes.

Now, let's add an absolutely positioned `div` to show the owner's balance. Add the following line right beneath the opening `body` tag:

```
<div class="absolute right-1 top-1 tc pt4 left f5 pb3 bg-black-80 w4
    h4 shadow-2 br4 white">You have
  <div class="f3 mt3">
    <span id="accountBalance" class="b"></span>
    TodoCoin
  </div>
</div>
```

You'll notice that it does not specify your balance of `10000 TodoCoin`, but rather just looks like this:

This is because you have not written any JavaScript to connect to your smart contract's data yet. That will come very shortly.

And lastly, let's add a `div` to represent the transaction status:

```
<div id="transactionStatus" class="pt4"></div>
```

Your whole screen should now look like this:

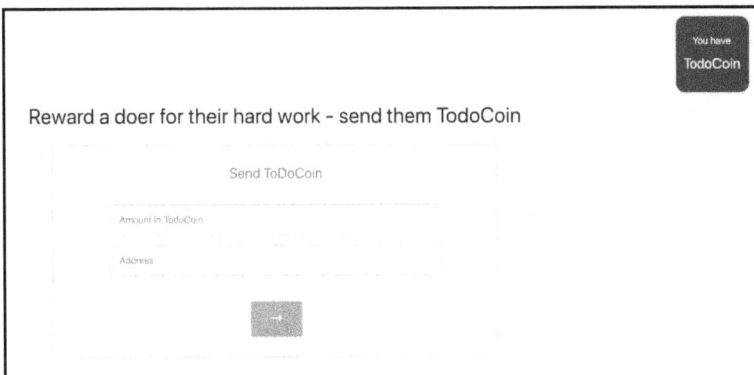

And; your `index.html` file should look like the one here: https://github.com/PacktPublishing/Truffle-Quick-Start-Guide/blob/master/chapter1/app/index.html.

Let's write some JavaScript

Now, let's write some JavaScript and make use of the `web3` library. Don't worry if you are not familiar with `web3`, you will see more of that in Chapter 2, *Web3 and Solidity in Truffle*. For now, you will interact with `web3` just enough to get a fully working *Dapp*.

In `app.js`, paste the following code:

```
import { default as Web3} from 'web3';
import { default as contract } from 'truffle-contract'
import taskMasterArtifacts from '../../build/contracts/TaskMaster.json'
```

By pasting in the preceding code, you just imported the following:

- Your CSS file, for Webpack bundling and build purposes (not important for now)
- `web3`—this is to connect with Ethereum blockchains
- `truffle-contract`—an Ethereum contract abstraction for the browser that allows you to invoke public smart contract methods from plain old JavaScript objects
- A JSON representation of your `TaskMaster.sol` contract file

Why do we import a JSON file and not a Solidity file?

Before you deploy a contract to a blockchain network, your contract needs to be compiled into bytecode understood by the **EVM** (**Ethereum Virtual Machine**), and provide an **ABI** (application binary interface). The ABI is the process for encoding your Solidity contract to be understood by the EVM, and this file is in a JSON format. When you run compile, you will notice that a build folder is created along with JSON data of your contracts.

Under our `import` statements, let's declare and initialize a few variables:

```
var TaskMaster = contract(taskMasterArtifacts);
var ownerAccount;
```

We use `contract` to get the JavaScript abstraction of our contract. This is necessary to call public functions such as `getBalance` and `reward`. As you can see, `contract` is a function that accepts your contract's ABI JSON file.

Next, we need to tell `web3` which blockchain network to connect to:

```
window.addEventListener('load', function() {
  window.web3 = new Web3(new
Web3.providers.HttpProvider("http://127.0.0.1:9545"));
});
```

On the load event of the window, we:

- Set `web3` as a window object and give it our localhost (`http://127.0.0.1:9545`) as the blockchain network provider
- You will learn more about `web3` providers in subsequent chapters

The moral of this story is that `web3` requires a blockchain provider to allow us to interact with the said blockchain on the frontend. Notice that when you enter `truffle develop`, it takes you to a console that looks like this:

```
Truffle Develop started at http://localhost:9545/

Accounts:
(0) 0x627306090abab3a6e1400e9345bc60c78a8bef57
(1) 0xf17f52151ebef6c7334fad080c5704d77216b732
(2) 0xc5fdf4076b8f3a5357c5e395ab970b5b54098fef
(3) 0x821aea9a577a9b44299b9c15c88cf3087f3b5544
(4) 0x0d1d4e623d10f9fba5db95830f7d3839406c6af2
(5) 0x2932b7a2355d6fecc4b5c0b6bd44cc31df247a2e
(6) 0x2191ef87e392377ec08e7c08eb105ef5448eced5
(7) 0x0f4f2ac550a1b4e2280d04c21cea7ebd822934b5
(8) 0x6330a553fc93768f612722bb8c2ec78ac90b3bbc
(9) 0x5aeda56215b167893e80b4fe645ba6d5bab767de

Private Keys:
(0) c87509a1c067bbde78beb793e6fa76530b6382a4c0241e5e4a9ec0a0f44dc0d3
(1) ae6ae8e5ccbfb04590405997ee2d52d2b330726137b875053c36d94e974d162f
(2) 0dbbe8e4ae425a6d2687f1a7e3ba17bc98c673636790f1b8ad91193c05875ef1
(3) c88b703fb08cbea894b6aeff5a544fb92e78a18e19814cd85da83b71f772aa6c
(4) 388c684f0ba1ef5017716adb5d21a053ea8e90277d0868337519f97bede61418
(5) 659cbb0e2411a44db63778987b1e22153c086a95eb6b18bdf89de078917abc63
(6) 82d052c865f5763aad42add438569276c00d3d88a2d062d36b2bae914d58b8c8
(7) aa3680d5d48a8283413f7a108367c7299ca73f553735860a87b08f39395618b7
(8) 0f62d96d6675f32685bbdb8ac13cda7c23436f63efbb9d07700d8669ff12b7c4
(9) 8d5366123cb560bb606379f90a0bfd4769eecc0557f1b362dcae9012b548b1e5
```

Truffle for Decentralized Applications

In particular, notice the statement at the top: `Truffle Develop started at http://localhost:9545/`. This is the same URL and port that we specified in the following code block.

Also, notice that in our local blockchain we have nine accounts with their respective private keys. These nine accounts are all the accounts in our mini, private, and local blockchain:

```
window.web3 = new Web3(
    new Web3.providers.HttpProvider("http://127.0.0.1:9545")
);
```

Essentially, we are using a local copy of a mock blockchain.

Next, let's create a global object called `TaskMasterApp` to encapsulate logic involving listening for click events and performing DOM updates. Above the `web3` code, paste the following code:

```
window.TaskMasterApp = {};
```

Our `TaskMaster` object also needs to be made aware of the current `web3` provider. Let's add a method to `TaskMasterApp`:

```
setWeb3Provider: function() {
  TaskMaster.setProvider(web3.currentProvider);
}
```

We'll call this method `setWeb3Provider`, because we want to set a provider for `web3`.

You can now paste the following as the final step inside the `load` callback, after setting a provider for `web3`:

```
TaskMasterApp.setWeb3Provider();
```

Go to `https://localhost:8080/#/`. You should see no errors, and nothing in the console.

Next, we should get all accounts associated with the current `web3` provider, and set our `ownerAccount` variable to the first account. Let's add another method to `TaskMasterApp`:

```
getAccounts: function () {
  var self = this;
  web3.eth.getAccounts(function(error, accounts) {
    if (error != null) {
      alert("Sorry, something went wrong. We couldn't fetch your accounts.");
      return;
```

```
    }
    if (!accounts.length) {
       alert("Sorry, no errors, but we couldn't get any accounts - Make sure
your Ethereum client is configured correctly.");
       return;
    }
    ownerAccount = accounts[0];
  })
},
```

As you can see, we are getting the first account and setting it to our `ownerAccount` variable. Also, you'll notice that `web3.eth.getAccounts` is not the most elegantly designed, as it requires a callback function. In later chapters, we will work with promises to avoid callback hell.

You'll notice that we don't use ES6 syntax here (`var` instead of `const`, and so forth). This is because we are still writing in vanilla JavaScript.

Remember, we are only focusing on one thing at a time. Once we get the fundamentals of Truffle, web3, and Solidity down solidly, we'll start looking into modern JavaScript technologies such as Angular, React, and Node.

Inside of the window load function, after we call `TaskMasterApp.setWeb3Provider()`, let's make a call to get all accounts:

```
TaskMasterApp.getAccounts();
```

Now that we have accounts, we can find a way to populate our status `div`. Let's create a method on `TaskMasterApp` called `refreshAccountBalance`. We are calling it `refreshAccountBalance` because we'll invoke this method again when we send ether to a doer to see the DOM update instantly. For this reason, we opt for a more descriptive name than, say, `setAccountBalance`:

```
    refreshAccountBalance: function() {
      var self = this;

      TaskMaster.deployed()
        .then(function(taskMasterInstance) {
          return taskMasterInstance.getBalance.call(ownerAccount, {
            from: ownerAccount
          });
        }).then(function(value) {
```

Truffle for Decentralized Applications

```
        document.getElementById("accountBalance").innerHTML =
          value.valueOf();
        document.getElementById("accountBalance").style.color =
        "white";
      }).catch(function(e) {
        console.log(e);
      });
    }
```

Notice how we call `TaskMaster.deployed()`. This returns a promise that resolves to a usable instance.

Then, we can get the owner's balance by calling `taskMasterInstance.getBalance.call(account, {from: account})`.

In this case, `msg.sender` is the owner's account.

Let's see it in action. Inside `TaskMasterApp.getAccounts`, add the following line of code at the very end:

```
    self.refreshAccountBalance();
```

Now, you should see the balance updated on the DOM:

Now, let's create a method to reward a doer:

```
    rewardDoer: function() {
      var self = this;

      var todoCoinReward = +document.getElementById("todoCoinReward").value;
      var doer = document.getElementById("doer").value;

      TaskMaster.deployed()
        .then(function(taskMasterInstance) {
          return taskMasterInstance.reward(doer, todoCoinReward, {
```

Chapter 1

```
      from: ownerAccount
    });
  }).then(function() {
    self.refreshAccountBalance();
  }).catch(function(e) {
    console.log(e);
  });
}
```

We invoke `rewardDoer` and pass in a receiver and amount, and the account that initiates this call is `ownerAccount`. That's `msg.sender`. Once the promise resolves, we refresh the owner's balance.

We need to attach a click handler on our `button` too:

```
<button
  class="white pa3 ph4 bg-green br2 f3 b pointer"
  onclick="TaskMasterApp.rewardDoer()">→
</button>
```

Enter any reward amount you wish, and see the balance decrease by that amount. Also, make sure you enter a valid Ethereum address.

I transferred `22` TodoCoin to `0x85db1e131b6c5c0c7eec98fed091a441ed856424`. Here's what my screen looks like:

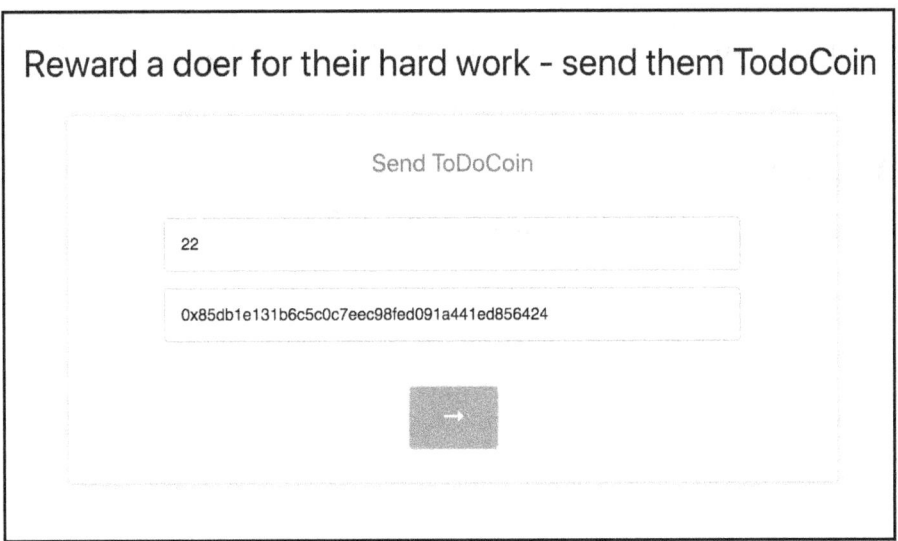

Once I submitted, my balance refreshed:

Now, let's see one last method involving `TaskMasterApp` to update our status `div`:

```
updateTransactionStatus: function(statusMessage) {
    document.getElementById("transactionStatus").innerHTML = statusMessage;
}
```

Now, you can view the transaction status on the UI. Send some more TodoCoin to a doer, and look at the bottom of the screen. You should see the following words:

`Transaction complete!`

References

Christian, Brian, and Tom Griffiths. *Algorithms to Live By*. Henry Holt and Company, 2016.

Summary

That's it. Congratulations on building your first *Dapp*; you've covered a lot of ground here! You can find the fully working *Dapp* that we built in this chapter over here: `https://github.com/PacktPublishing/Truffle-Quick-Start-Guide/tree/master/chapter1`.

If you've noticed, we haven't yet included proper error handling or unit tests, or migrations. We will cover all of that in subsequent chapters. I hope you enjoyed building this mini *Dapp*, and that you now have a solid understanding of the power of Truffle.

See you in `Chapter 2`, *Web3 and Solidity in Truffle*.

2
Web3 and Solidity in Truffle

This chapter will introduce you to web3, and its related APIs and uses in Truffle. You will gain an understanding of the fundamentals of web3 and how it is used in Truffle to connect to and help develop blockchain and/or smart contract-based applications. Moreover, this chapter will give you a brief refresher about Solidity, including functions, data types, visibility specifiers, and events.

Specifically, you will:

- Learn and understand the reasons for the use of web3 in an isolated environment in Truffle
- Learn and understand the reasons for the use of web3 in Truffle
- Learn and understand the use of various types of functions and data types in Solidity
- Learn and understand when and why events are used
- Learn and understand how to use the appropriate type and visibility specifier when defining a function

Technical requirements

You will be required to have basic knowledge of JavaScript and web development as well as Ethereum/blockchain. Finally, to use the Git repository of this book, the user needs to install Git.

The code files of this chapter can be found on GitHub:
https://github.com/PacktPublishing/Truffle-Quick-Start-Guide/tree/master/Chapter02

Check out the following video to see the code in action:
http://bit.ly/2tiC7cu

What is web3?

We mentioned web3 briefly in `Chapter 1`, *Truffle for Decentralized Applications*, and we even used it without fully understanding it. The purpose of `Chapter 1`, *Truffle for Decentralized Applications*, was to get a fully functional and working *Dapp* on a local blockchain so you could understand the power of Truffle.

Now, it's time to get more granular.

Web3 is a collection of APIs that allows JavaScript to access blockchain-based data and perform common Ethereum functions such as getting all accounts in a particular network, getting the balance of an account, or getting the particular block number.

Let's take a look at some examples:

```
var balance =
web3.eth.getBalance("0x407d73d8a49eeb85d32cf465507dd71d507100c1");
console.log(balance); // instanceof BigNumber
console.log(balance.toString(10)); // '1000000000000'
console.log(balance.toNumber()); // 1000000000000
```

The `web3.eth.getBalance` function takes a string as an input. Particularly, this string should be a valid Ethereum address. The example simply shown is just a randomly generated address with a fake balance, made purely for the purposes of this example.

You'll notice that we don't use ES6 syntax here (`var` instead of `const`, and so forth). This is because we are still writing in vanilla JavaScript.

Remember, we are only focusing on one thing at a time. Once we get the fundamentals of Truffle, web3, and Solidity down solidly, we'll start looking into modern JavaScript frameworks and libraries such as Angular, Vue, and React.

Let's take another example:

```
web3.eth.getAccounts(callback(error, result){ ... })
```

Here, we are trying to get all the accounts of *a particular network*. As you can see, the function takes a callback as an argument.

To see this function in action, we need to tell web3 about the blockchain network we want to connect to. Remember when we attached a network provider to web3 in Chapter 1, *Truffle for Decentralized Applications*?

In Chapter 1, *Truffle for Decentralized Applications*, we connected to a local, test blockchain by running truffle develop inside of our root project folder. This worked because we were inside of a truffle project.

But now we're not! What if we only want to see how web3 works? Remember, to get a solid grip of web3, it's helpful to play with it in an *isolated* environment before integrating it with Truffle. To achieve this, we'll need another way of having localhost on port 8545 connected to a local blockchain. That's where Ganache-CLI comes in.

Ganache-CLI

Ganache-CLI is an Ethereum client that enables you to connect to a local blockchain for testing your decentralized application. You'll see more of Ethereum clients in Chapter 3, *Choosing an Ethereum Client*, but for now, just know that it allows us to connect to a local Ethereum blockchain (localhost:8545). Here, we are just using Ganache-CLI to create a local blockchain on localhost:8545.

Let's install ganache-cli with the following command:

```
npm install ganache-cli -g
```

Then, run it. In a separate terminal window/tab, run ganache-cli.

Web3 and Solidity in Truffle

That's it. In the terminal that you ran `ganache-cli`, you should see a very familiar screen:

As you can see, it's a window—our test blockchain with the accounts and their private keys listed. You can also see it connected to and listening on `localhost:8545`. Your accounts may be different. Remember, this blockchain is local, so mine is probably different from yours.

Chapter 2

Great. Now that we have `ganache-cli`, let's create a JavaScript file to see `web3` in action. Back in our original tab, perform the following:

1. Create a new folder called `chapter2`
2. Go inside the `chapter2` folder
3. Create a file called `web3-playground.js`

In the file, make the necessary imports, and specify our localhost as the provider:

```
var Web3 = require('web3'); // gets the Web3 object, which is a function constructor
var web3 = new Web3(); // instantiate Web3 to get a new object

web3 = new Web3(new Web3.providers.HttpProvider("http://localhost:8545"));
```

Now, the `web3` object knows about our blockchain network, so let's get all of the accounts.

Add this piece of code at the top of your `web3-playground.js` file:

```
web3.eth.getAccounts()
  .then(function (accounts) {
    console.log(JSON.stringify(accounts, null, 2));
  })
  .catch(function (error) {
    console.error(error);
  });
```

`web3.eth.getAccounts()` returns a promise that once resolved, will hold an array of accounts.

To run this file, go back to your terminal. Inside the `chapter2` folder, run the following:

- `node web3-playground.js`—this command tells the node to run your `web3-playground.js` file
- Make sure `ganache-cli` is still running in the other window/tab; we always need to be connected to a blockchain network

> If you want the node to rerun automatically after every single modification in your `web3-playground.js` file, you can install nodemon. Nodemon monitors your application for changes and automatically restarts the server.
>
> Once installed, you can simply run `nodemon web3-playground.js`.

After executing the preceding commands, in your terminal console, you should see the following output:

```
[
  "0x6ef727d2AE240B027e7174CAd877586C8f499c21",
  "0x1f4A302E5e2513728dd19978289C0EB6d28D8980",
  "0xDccA5AC58497C032BA5EbB0F997736c6334e6ae6",
  "0x9efA60C7721C39e25fa5008A79A85b0a34E2fbC0",
  "0x586a166896D9c4B44F8c1713eC319DbDcA6Dec07",
  "0xCAB8C28553Aa49b282b8245ffc20234294a27336",
  "0x88632F8da98e4f3a4a62d1621D569855F92cA13E",
  "0x3d5351216EFb9d4Df0E0dcD8DcBa0a630E7255a0",
  "0xC788D5f59Adf287fFA1a7AbbC4F075F1c17df1ff",
  "0x737eCf7D5DfCD6a4384de3C9cae7D7d77993f6D4"
]
```

Yours will be different. However, these accounts should match (not necessarily in order) with the accounts shown in the `ganache-cli` terminal.

Great! Let's play some more. Let's get the `wei` balance of an account.

After the `getAccounts` promise, add a `then` to get the balance of the first account. Then, resolve it, and print the result out to the console:

```
web3.eth.getAccounts()
  .then(function (accounts) {
    console.log(JSON.stringify(accounts, null, 2));
    return accounts;
  })
  .then(function (accounts) {
    var firstAccount = accounts[0];
    return web3.eth.getBalance(firstAccount);
  })
  .then(function (accountBalance) {
    console.log('balance in wei: ', accountBalance);
    return accountBalance;
  })
  .catch(function (error) {
    console.error(error);
  });
```

You should now see `balance in wei: 100000000000000000000` in the console. As you may have guessed, `web3.eth.getBalance` returns a promise that resolves to an integer.

Nice! We are getting the hang of web3's power now. Let's try a few more things.

You may have wondered if we can represent our balances in `wei` and/or `ether`, as that's where the `fromWei` function is useful.

At the end of your `web3-playground.js` file, inside the promise resolution of `web3.eth.getBalance`, add another line to convert the balance to `ether`:

```
console.log('balance in ether: ', web3.utils.fromWei(accountBalance, 'ether'));
```

You should see a new line in your terminal output: `balance in ether: 100`.

As you can see, one `ether` is equal to 1,000,000,000,000,000,000 Wei! That's a lot of Wei, and for this reason, Wei is the smallest denomination and base unit of ether.

You'll notice that that the `fromWei` function is on the `utils` object of `web3`. This may be different for you depending on the version of `web3` you have installed.

Hence, pay attention to your version and consult its corresponding documentation for its proper uses. The version of `web3` we are using for this tutorial is `^1.0.0-beta.30`

Good job! We've created a `web3-playground.js` file where we are free to write and play with `web3` commands in an isolated environment. Your full `web3-playground.js` file should look like the one here: https://github.com/PacktPublishing/Truffle-Quick-Start-Guide/blob/master/chapter2/web3-playground.js.

There many more features of `web3`, so take your time and add more to your `web3-playground.js` file. It's there to help you play and learn.

Web3 in Truffle

Now that we have a clear understanding of `web3` in an isolated environment, it's time to get out of our comfort zone and see how it interacts with Truffle. We've already seen a bit of this in `Chapter 1`, *Truffle for Decentralized Applications*.

Let's refer back to our `app.js` file under `chapter1/app/javascripts/` (https://github.com/PacktPublishing/Truffle-Quick-Start-Guide/blob/master/chapter1/app/javascripts/app.js).

Let's see how we import `web3`:

```
import { default as Web3} from 'web3';
```

Now, let's see how we set the blockchain network provider for `web3`:

```
window.web3 = new Web3(new
Web3.providers.HttpProvider("http://127.0.0.1:9545"));
```

Remember how we simply glossed over this in Chapter 1, *Truffle for Decentralized Applications*? Hopefully, you now have a better understanding of what's going on here. Since we don't have MetaMask or Mist installed in our browser (you may, but it's not needed), we simply *fallback* to our local blockchain.

Now, let's see how we got all of the accounts inside of our test blockchain:

```
getAccounts: function () {
  var self = this;
  web3.eth.getAccounts(function(error, accounts) {
    if (error != null) {
      alert("Sorry, something went wrong. We couldn't fetch your
        accounts.");
      return;
    }

    if (!accounts.length) {
      alert("Sorry, no errors, but we couldn't get any accounts -
      Make sure your Ethereum client is configured correctly.");
      return;
    }

    ownerAccount = accounts[0];
    self.refreshAccountBalance();
  });
},
...
```

Chapter 2

Of course, we are still stuck in ugly callback land here. At the time of the writing of this book, the version of web3 that is installed with Truffle does not support promises. There are a few ways to solve this problem, one of which is to play with your file configurations. You can check that out here, a recently closed GitHub issue: `https://github.com/trufflesuite/truffle-contract/issues/56`.

The quicker way is to use a utility function to *promisify* all callbacks. That is, pass a callback into this utility function and return the promise-friendly version. We will see this in `Chapter 3`, *Choosing an Ethereum Client for Your Dapp*.

We call `web3.eth.getAccounts` and simply assign the returned accounts to our variables inside of the callback. I hope this is all looking clearer to you now.

And that's it. Those are all of the occurrences where we used `web3` inside our mini *Dapp*. As you can see, `web3` behaves the same way inside of the Truffle environment.

Solidity – a refresher

This is by no means a comprehensive tutorial on Solidity. This section will give you enough knowledge to build a fully functional Truffle *Dapp*. For more information on Solidity, the documentation is very handy; check it out here: `https://solidity.readthedocs.io/en/v0.4.21/`.

If you already have a good grasp of Solidity, you can skip the rest of this chapter and move on to `Chapter 3`, *Choosing an Ethereum Client for Your Dapp*.

In this section, we will cover Solidity basics. Further, you will find subsections for important components of Solidity. Let's start with our first component—data types.

Data types

Solidity, just like any other language, has some data types. Of them, let's first take a look at some *value* types. The value types in Solidity are as follows:

- bool
- int (defaults at 256 bits)
- uint (defaults at 256 bits)
- address (defaults at 160 bits); it includes, but is not limited to, the following functions:
    - balance
    - transfer (uint)

To hold groups of data, there are also arrays, structs, and mappings. However, these three types are fundamentally different from one another. Let's take a look.

Arrays

Arrays in Solidity are:

- Passed by reference
- Returned by value
- Zero-based indexed

For fixed-size arrays, the available value types are `bytes1` to `bytes32`, in *multiple-of-eight lengths* (`bytes8`, `bytes16`, and so on). For dynamically sized arrays, the available types are bytes and strings.

Structs

Here are some facts about structs in Solidity:

- They are passed by reference
- They allow you to group related data into a single entity:

```
struct Task {
    uint id;
    string name;
    string description;
    uint ethReward;
}
```

- They can only be returned from a function for internal calls

Mapping

A mapping in Solidity:

- Is a structure to associate a key with a value—similar to hash maps or dictionaries in other languages
- Has a default value of 0, associated to each key

Visibility specifiers

 A variable is *internal* by default. However, its visibility can be overridden with `private` or `public` visibility specifiers.

Here are the visibility specifiers in Solidity:

- `private`:
    - Can be *read from* and *written to* *only* within the contract it has been declared in
- `public`:
    - Can be *read from any* contract but *written to* only within the contract it has been declared in and the children of that contract
- `internal`:
    - Can be *read from* and *written to* only within the contract it has been declared in and the children of that contract
    - The default visibility

Functions

This section will cover enough Solidity function knowledge for you to build a fully functional Truffle *Dapp*.

If you wish to gain a deeper understanding of Solidity functions and learn concepts such as function signatures, internal/external functions, and more, a great resource is http://solidity.readthedocs.io/en/develop/contracts.html#functions.

The most fundamental use of a function is in the constructor of a contract. We did this in Chapter 1, *Truffle for Decentralized Applications*.

```
function TaskMaster() public {
    balances[msg.sender] = 10000;
    owner = msg.sender;
}
```

The first thing you may notice is the public visibility specifier. This is not to be confused with the variable visibility specifiers we just covered. Functions have their *own* visibility specifiers; here they are:

- private:
    - Invokable from *only* within the contract they are defined in
- public:
    - Invokable from *any* contract
    - The default visibility
- internal:
    - Invokable from *only* within the contract it has been declared in and the children of that contract
- external:
    - Invokable from *any* contract
    - Arguments are read directly from calldata rather than memory
    - Costs less gas than a public function

Chapter 2

We won't focus on external and internal functions for the remainder of this book. This list is just to give you an idea of all the visibility specifiers available to you.

For more information of internal and external functions, this link is helpful: `http://solidity.readthedocs.io/en/develop/contracts.html#functions`.

Let's take a look at the constructor again. What else do you notice:

```
function TaskMaster() public {
    balances[msg.sender] = 10000;
    owner = msg.sender;
}
```

We use the magic variable `msg.sender`.

It's not exactly magic. `msg.sender` is among the few special variables you will have access to within a Solidity function.

Here is a list of *some* important special variables.

- `msg.sender`:
  - The address of the account/contract that called the function—`address`
- `msg.value`:
  - The number of `wei` sent with the function call or message—`uint`
- `now`:
  - The current block timestamp—`uint`

You can find a comprehensive list of special variables here: `http://solidity.readthedocs.io/en/develop/units-and-global-variables.html`.

Let's take a look at another function we wrote:

```
function reward(address doer, uint rewardAmount)
    public
    isOwner()
    hasSufficientFunds(rewardAmount)
```

Web3 and Solidity in Truffle

```
        returns(bool sufficientFunds)
    {
        balances[msg.sender] -= rewardAmount;
        balances[doer] += rewardAmount;
        return sufficientFunds;
    }
```

You'll notice the function has been modified with `isOwner()` and `hasSufficientFunds(rewardAmount)`.

What does this mean? `isOwner` and `hasSufficientFunds` are examples of function modifiers.

Function modifiers

Modifiers are just functions that are typically called before the function they are *modifying*. In our example, the `isOwner` and `hasSufficientFunds` modifiers are called before the body of reward is executed.

Let's peek inside one of the modifiers:

```
    modifier isOwner() {
        require(msg.sender == owner);
        _;
    }
```

Notice `require`.

You can think of `require` as similar to its namesake, where it requires the condition inside of it to evaluate to `true`. If the condition inside of the `require` evaluates to `false`, all state changes will be undone and the remaining gas will be returned to the caller.

Here, we are *requiring* that the `msg.sender` is indeed the owner of the contract. If they are, and if the `hasSufficientFunds` modifier passes, then we can run the code inside the body of `reward`.

And that's precisely what `_;` means, too. It is a special character that returns the flow of execution to the original function (`reward`, in this case).

Let's take one last look at the `reward` function before we move on:

```
    function reward(address doer, uint rewardAmount)
        public
        isOwner()
```

```
    hasSufficientFunds(rewardAmount)
    returns(bool sufficientFunds)
{
    balances[msg.sender] -= rewardAmount;
    balances[doer] += rewardAmount;
    return sufficientFunds;
}
```

Notice `returns(bool sufficientFunds)`.

In Solidity, you can (and should) specify a return type of a function. You can also name your return types and simply return them via the same name, as shown here with `sufficientFunds` being the boolean variable being returned. This option to name your return types is for readability purposes.

> The keyword `payable` is also a modifier for a function. `payable` allows a function to receive ether.

Function types

Let's look at the `getBalance` function that we created in Chapter 1, *Truffle for Decentralized Applications*.

```
function getBalance(address addr) public view returns(uint) {
    return balances[addr];
}
```

Notice `view`.

`view` is one of the few *types* functions you can specify in Solidity for a function. The function types are:

- `view`:
    - Does *not* allow the function to modify contract state, recieve, or send ether
    - Is the keyword replacement for `constant` (`view` should be used in place of `constant`)
- `pure`

- Does not allow the function to modify contract state, or recieve or send ether
- Does not allow the function to read from the environment or state

 You can find more information on the `pure` and `view` functions here: http://solidity.readthedocs.io/en/develop/contracts.html#functions.

Events

The last element of Solidity we will refresh is events. Put simply, events can be emitted anytime in a Solidity function, and they can be listened to from JavaScript.

Here is a simple example of an event being defined and emitted. Suppose we have a contract that transfers `ether` to a specified address:

```
pragma solidity ^0.4.17;

contract SimpleTransfer {
    uint public contractBalance;
    // Define the event
    event LogTransfer(address recipient);

    function SimpleTransfer() public payable {
        contractBalance = msg.value;
    }

    function sendEther(address recipient) public payable returns(bool
        success) {
        require(contractBalance > msg.value);
        LogTransfer(recipient);
        recipient.transfer(msg.value);
        return success;
    }
}
```

Notice how we define the event: `event LogTransfer(address recipient);`.

Then, we emit it inside of the `sendEther` function:

```
LogTransfer(recipient);
```

That's it.

 As mentioned earlier, you can get the event logs in JavaScript. We'll cover this in Chapter 3, *Choosing an Ethereum Client for Your Dapp*.

Summary

Great job. We've covered a lot in this chapter.

Just as we did with web3, the best way to learn or catch up on Solidity is to play with it inside of an *isolated* environment. I've created a file for you called solidity-playground.sol. You can find it here: https://github.com/PacktPublishing/Truffle-Quick-Start-Guide/blob/master/chapter2/solidity-playground.sol. This contains the same SimpleTransfer contract. It's for you to play with, add/alter functions, and so on—it's all yours. You can use an online Solidity IDE called Remix (https://remix.ethereum.org) to run your contract.

See you in Chapter 3, *Choosing an Ethereum Client for Your Dapp*, where you will learn how to interact with various Ethereum clients and choose the correct one for your Dapp.

3
Choosing an Ethereum Client for Your Dapp

This chapter will give you a chance to integrate all of your newly learned skills and apply them to our real-world smart contract. You will expand on the mini Dapp you built in Chapter 1, *Truffle for Decentralized Applications*. This chapter will introduce you to various Ethereum clients, highlight the use case for each one, and show you how to integrate each Ethereum client with your Truffle application.

Specifically, you will:

- Learn and understand how to connect with Geth, Parity, and Ganache
- Learn and understand how to choose the appropriate Ethereum client to use with your Truffle Dapp
- See how these three Ethereum clients interact with Truffle

Technical requirements

You will be required to have basic knowledge of JavaScript and web development as well as Ethereum/blockchain. Finally, to use the Git repository of this book, the user needs to install Git.

The code files of this chapter can be found on GitHub:
https://github.com/PacktPublishing/Truffle-Quick-Start-Guide/tree/master/Chapter03

Check out the following video to see the code in action:
http://bit.ly/2MNdUmL

Geth, Parity, and Ganache

Geth, Parity, and Ganache are three of the most common Ethereum clients you will encounter as you build decentralized applications. You've already briefly seen how Ganache works by using `ganache-cli` in the second chapter. And, to be honest, you've seen most if it already! This chapter will touch on the last few bits of Ganache, and it will take a shallow dive into Geth and Parity to give you an idea of the power of the most widely used Ethereum clients.

 Although we will briefly cover Geth and Parity, we will mainly focus on Ganache for the rest of this book as it allows you to get a Truffle Dapp up and running quickly, and with the least development pain.

What is an Ethereum client?

An Ethereum client allows you to access the Ethereum blockchain network, verify transactions, mine blocks, and more. Which blockchain network? You can connect to any Ethereum blockchain network, as long as you specify it. Each client has its own special rules and functions that dictate how you connect to a specific Ethereum network.

Here is a diagram to help you understand where an Ethereum client fits in to the large picture.

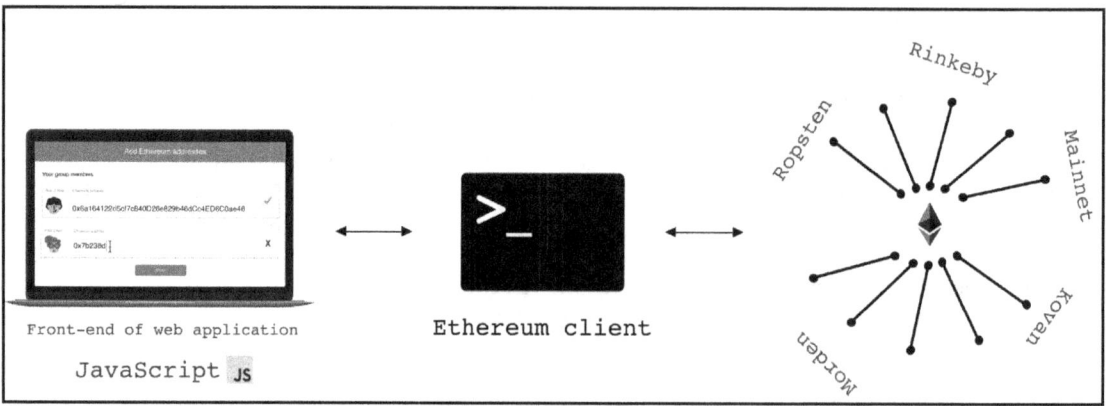

When you read about blockchains on the internet, you will often come across the term `nodes`. Well, you can think of an Ethereum client as a fancy term for a `node`.

That is, an Ethereum client allows you to access an Ethereum network, verify transactions, and do much more.

How do these clients differ? The easiest way for us to find out is to dive into and play with each client. Let's start with Geth.

Geth

Geth is one of the most powerful Ethereum clients out there, and you'll soon see why. Its name, Geth, originates from the fact that it is an Ethereum client built in *Go*, `G + eth = Geth`. It is open source, and you can find its code on GitHub here: `https://github.com/ethereum/go-ethereum`.

As you will see on its GitHub, Geth is described as the Official golang implementation of the Ethereum protocol. Don't be confused by such language; Ethereum just exposes a set of protocols that, if implemented, will allow you to get and post data from it.

How does Geth work?

Before we see how Geth interacts with Truffle, the best way to learn about Geth is inside an isolated environment. Head over to `https://github.com/ethereum/go-ethereum/wiki/Building-Ethereum` to see installation instructions.

Make sure to create a new account, as mentioned later in the instructions, with `geth account new`.

Choosing an Ethereum Client for Your Dapp

 When you go through the installation steps, notice how you have to create an account with a password. This account that you create will be your home account inside of the `geth` environment, also known as your `coinbase`.

It will be the account which ETH rewards will be transferred to if you were to mine ether. Don't worry if this sounds confusing, we're about to cover this below.

Once you have `geth` installed, simply run the following command in your terminal to build a `geth` environment inside of your computer:

```
make geth
```

Great! We've installed and built `geth`, but we still have no idea what it does. Let's take a look at the sections below to play with and understand the power of `geth`.

The power of Geth

Firstly, `geth` allows us to do what we have done in the past with `ganache-cli`. That is, `geth` allows you to:

- Connect to an Ethereum network of your choice
- Get all of your accounts in a network
- Get the balance of any one of your accounts
- Transfer funds
- Do much, much more

We will cover the basics, but to learn more, you can check out the Wiki here: https://github.com/ethereum/go-ethereum/wiki/geth.

To access the main Ethereum network inside of the `geth` environment, run the following command inside your terminal:

```
geth console
```

As specified on the GitHub page, running `geth console` will:

- Start up the interactive JavaScript console built inside of `geth`. This JavaScript console allows you to invoke all `web3` functions that you have already seen in the previous chapters.

Once you run `geth console`, your console will look something similar to this:

```
INFO [03-22|17:44:43] Maximum peer count                       ETH=25 LES=0 total=25
INFO [03-22|17:44:43] Starting peer-to-peer node               instance=Geth/v1.8.2-stable/darwin-amd64/go1.10
INFO [03-22|17:44:43] Allocated cache and file handles         database=/Users/nikhilwins/Library/Ethereum/geth/chaindata cache=768 handles=1024
INFO [03-22|17:44:44] Initialised chain configuration          config="{ChainID: 1 Homestead: 1150000 DAO: 1920000 DAOSupport: true EIP150: 2463000 EIP155: 2675000 EIP158: 2675000 Byzantium: 4370000 Constantinople: <nil> Engine: ethash}"
INFO [03-22|17:44:44] Disk storage enabled for ethash caches   dir=/Users/nikhilwins/Library/Ethereum/geth/ethash count=3
INFO [03-22|17:44:44] Disk storage enabled for ethash DAGs     dir=/Users/nikhilwins/.ethash count=2
INFO [03-22|17:44:44] Initialising Ethereum protocol           versions="[63 62]" network=1
INFO [03-22|17:44:44] Loaded most recent local header          number=1008264 hash=6a9a62…9d3929 td=7239327024842070734
INFO [03-22|17:44:44] Loaded most recent local full block      number=0        hash=d4e567…cb8fa3 td=17179869184
INFO [03-22|17:44:44] Loaded most recent local fast block      number=991049   hash=9bbf93…6d46ad td=7029237091804882068
INFO [03-22|17:44:44] Upgrading chain index                    type=bloombits percentage=92
INFO [03-22|17:44:44] Loaded local transaction journal         transactions=0 dropped=0
INFO [03-22|17:44:44] Regenerated local transaction journal    transactions=0 accounts=0
INFO [03-22|17:44:44] Starting P2P networking
INFO [03-22|17:44:46] UDP listener up                          self=enode://e6f95d133b86c25fe43502f65c249a30903484929b24c9dbbe789a2089667f19045b6f4cb1e9a10cea997ce9
```

This is equivalent to running `ganache-cli`, which results in a similar console, as you've seen in the previous chapters.

Choosing an Ethereum Client for Your Dapp

On the fourth INFO line, notice {ChainID: 1 ..}. ChainID refers to the current chain that we are on, and the main network has an ID of 1. In other words, we are connected to the main Ethereum network. You can view a list of other network (chain) IDs here: https://ethereum.stackexchange.com/questions/17051/how-to-select-a-network-id-or-is-there-a-list-of-network-ids.

> You'll notice that after running `geth console`, your terminal window has plenty of logs that keep running, and this can get a little frustrating when you are trying to run `web3` commands. Therefore, you can run w. This will prevent logs from continuously appearing in your console.

Good, we've got `geth` up and running now. Let's execute some `web3` commands and see how can we can use `geth` to interact with the main Ethereum network.

Common GETH actions

To get all of the accounts that you have in the network, simply run the following:

    web3.eth.accounts

You should see an output similar to this. It won't be the same account, of course:

    ["0xb1fa39f962682f8c85cdf1e21042712195a74b14"]

This is your home and current account, and is also known as your `coinbase`. Your `coinbase` is where your mining rewards get transferred to. Let's directly access our `coinbase`:

    web3.eth.coinbase

This should give you the following output:

    0xb1fa39f962682f8c85cdf1e21042712195a74b14

To get the balance of our `coinbase`, run the following command:

    web3.eth.getBalance(web3.eth.coinbase)

Your terminal output should show this:

    0

You have nothing. This is because you have not mined yet. We will briefly cover mining in the next chapter, but mining is still outside the realm of this book. You can learn more about mining in `geth` here: https://github.com/ethereum/go-ethereum/wiki/Mining.

To exit the `geth` console, simply run `exit`.

So, that's `geth` in a nutshell! In this section we:

- Connected to the main Ethereum network
- Displayed our accounts
- Displayed our `coinbase`
- Displayed the balance of our `coinbase`
- Exited the `geth` console

And, we did all of this thanks to `geth`'s JavaScript console that allowed us to use `web3`.

Now, let's turn our attention to Parity, an alternative Ethereum client.

Parity

Parity, like Geth, is an open source Ethereum client. You can find its code on GitHub here: https://github.com/paritytech/parity.
In that same link, you can find the installation and build instructions. Follow them according to your operating (OSX, Windows, and so on) and get ready to play around with Parity.

The power of Parity

Parity, like Geth, allows you to:

- Connect to an Ethereum network of your choice
- Get all of your accounts in a network
- Get the balance of any one of your accounts
- Transfer funds
- Do much, much more

Choosing an Ethereum Client for Your Dapp

To access the main Ethereum network inside of the `parity` environment, run the following command inside your Terminal:

`parity --geth`

Your Terminal window should now look similar to this:

```
2018-03-22 18:37:40  DB path /Users/nikhilwins/Library/Application Support/io.pari
ty.ethereum/chains/ethereum/db/906a34e69aec8c0d
2018-03-22 18:37:40  Path to dapps /Users/nikhilwins/Library/Application Support/i
o.parity.ethereum/dapps
2018-03-22 18:37:40  State DB configuration: fast
2018-03-22 18:37:40  Operating mode: passive
2018-03-22 18:37:40  Configured for Foundation using Ethash engine
2018-03-22 18:37:43  Updated conversion rate to Ξ1 = US$542.18 (219572140 wei/gas)
2018-03-22 18:37:46  Public node URL: enode://9b6f165951d72ed1a592f37af85c9a24a68a
d6a4b3844028bcda397c24f8348b5dbfc86568b0733896306c707a68836b59d8279ef92f7464dbdd06
6dbb6942b5@10.0.0.23:30303
2018-03-22 18:37:46  Syncing  #908951 acce…1798    0 blk/s   0 tx/s   0 Mgas/s
      0+    0 Qed  #908951  16/25 peers   74 KiB chain 66 MiB db 0 bytes queue 10
KiB sync  RPC:  0 conn,  0 req/s,   0 µs
2018-03-22 18:37:56  Syncing snapshot 4/807     #908951   22/25 peers   74 KiB chain
 66 MiB db 0 bytes queue 10 KiB sync  RPC:  0 conn,  0 req/s,   0 µs
2018-03-22 18:38:06  Syncing snapshot 7/807     #908951   25/25 peers   74 KiB chain
 66 MiB db 0 bytes queue 10 KiB sync  RPC:  0 conn,  0 req/s,   0 µs
2018-03-22 18:38:11  Syncing snapshot 11/807    #908951   25/25 peers   74 KiB chai
n 66 MiB db 0 bytes queue 10 KiB sync  RPC:  0 conn,  0 req/s,   0 µs
```

Why do we run this with the `--geth` flag? Unlike `geth`, Parity does not have a built-in JavaScript console where you can execute `web3` commands However, there is an option to run `parity` in a `geth` compatible mode. That is, inside of the `parity` environment, you can interact with the network using `web3`.

Good, we've got `parity` up and running now. Let's execute some `web3` commands and see how can we can use `parity` to interact with the main Ethereum network.

We need to tell `geth` to open a JavaScript console to use with our `parity` environment. In another Terminal window, run the following:

`geth attach`

Your Terminal window screen should now look like this:

```
Welcome to the Geth JavaScript console!

instance: Parity//v1.8.11-stable-21522ff-20180227/x86_
64-macos/rustc1.24.0
coinbase: 0x0000000000000000000000000000000000000000
at block: 875305 (Wed, 20 Jan 2016 10:20:22 +07)
 modules: eth:1.0 net:1.0 parity:1.0 parity_accounts:1
.0 parity_pubsub:1.0 personal:1.0 pubsub:1.0 rpc:1.0 s
ecretstore:1.0 shh:1.0 shh_pubsub:1.0 traces:1.0 web3:
1.0

>
```

Let's execute some `web3` commands and see how can we can use `parity` to interact with the main Ethereum network.

Common Parity actions

To get all accounts that you have in the network, simply run `web3.eth.accounts`.

You should see an output that is similar to this:

    []

That's because, in this network, you have not created any accounts for yourself. This is easy to fix; since we already created an account for `geth`, we can just import it! To import your accounts from `geth`, exit from the running Parity node and import your Geth keys.

To exit the `parity` console, simply run *Ctrl+C*.

To import your Geth keys, run the following command:

```
parity --import-geth-keys
```

Then, start Parity again:

```
parity --geth
```

Now run the same command to get your accounts:

```
web3.eth.accounts
```

You should now see the same accounts you saw in your `geth` environment. In my Terminal window, I see the following:

```
["0xb1fa39f962682f8c85cdf1e21042712195a74b14"]
```

Let's get our `coinbase`. Run the following command:

```
web3.eth.coinbase
```

This should give you something similar to this:

```
0xb1fa39f962682f8c85cdf1e21042712195a74b14
```

To get the balance of your coinbase, run this:

```
web3.eth.getBalance(web3.eth.coinbase)
```

You should see 0. Still 0, because it's the same account from our `geth` environment, and you haven't mined anything in `parity` or `geth`.

So, that's `parity` in a nutshell! In this section we:

- Connected to the main Ethereum network
- Displayed our accounts
- Displayed our coinbase
- Displayed the balance of our coinbase
- Exited the `parity` console

Now, let's turn our attention to the familiar `ganache-cli`, an Ethereum client for local development.

Ganache-CLI

Ganache-CLI is an Ethereum client that enables you to connect to a local blockchain for testing your decentralized application. It allows us to connect to a local Ethereum blockchain (`localhost:8545`). We use Ganache-CLI to create a local blockchain on `localhost:8545`.

If didn't already install `ganache-cli` in the previous chapter, you can do so now with the following command:

```
npm install ganache-cli -g
```

As usual, let's take a look at the sections below to play with and understand the power of `ganache-cli`.

The power of Ganache-CLI

Ganache-CLI allows you to:

- Create a local blockchain for testing
- Get all of your accounts in the local network
- Get the balance of any one of your accounts
- Transfer funds
- Do much, much more

To access the test Ethereum network inside of the `ganache-cli` environment, run the following command inside your terminal:

```
ganache-cli
```

Your Terminal window should now look similar to this:

```
Ganache CLI v6.0.3 (ganache-core: 2.0.2)

Available Accounts
==================
(0) 0xf54b8cccde4d31149ee537263a1db74d3491fdab
(1) 0x585a25b3aea6070bd54cf7a41295389857b5a77e
(2) 0xaba74ffdc21fcbf6ab9ef01430c2e3a96682b5dc
(3) 0xcb54122c72d897c06eebd3a0f57437a838f2cef4
(4) 0x07151274f09f3bceb1267672f4e7aaf363882f73
(5) 0x639b6dc466129b0e194892493948a03a23741a00
(6) 0xeb9bfaaf1a9ffb95829c2b8247b8843b56b820c9
(7) 0xba098ff569b884acd8ad55cadef00a578a28e8e3
(8) 0x345c38cead231a62053ec5608c2f130cba286a0d
(9) 0x33cb07aef13711737ddbe738095b55d53032a583

Private Keys
==================
(0) c746146664781fe70e7fc6f49e2f1c92c4073de1ac017d94b24785e5ef12e9fc
(1) 33a2456ce1225e5cccbf5991c0335297c5989b35eccf7972f48444ae21fd9d87
(2) 881c6669cbd026c22f58b3df9797b162298eaba9473e12eea942283e1e9ae123
(3) d77175332ecd82823dd8ae46734cd5df234c3f1f974497f9088b66455d36acec
(4) b39f191b4f9ca67d8867b5290b54639e8ee51fbb78731a73d4e11737a80f5742
(5) 87d3ed94391e8153641b88fa7bdd254f867433edd5ef598b9ce13543fc794460
(6) 1f80b799d8444a91b98f0511e13fc1b542adddde56f45db5d9b5db478438b1e4
(7) d455e25ba828252317ced615f8e0598a03bc3883441ad421b5a57ba76f963d45
(8) 8d877931f67859639dbb8e4f63c47e47c646348ee6a9a4cf2a645cef3d0c6667
(9) 99cc6268fd63284d86e4093eb24bfe3f2b97b9d8288b67545d9331b9894395b5

HD Wallet
==================
Mnemonic:      upper online similar budget claw punch arrest casino nurse yard alo
ne output
Base HD Path:  m/44'/60'/0'/0/{account_index}

Listening on localhost:8545
```

Let's execute some `web3` commands and see how can we can use `ganache-cli` to interact with our local Ethereum network.

Common Ganache-CLI actions

While `ganache-cli` is running in a Terminal window, in another terminal window, run:

node

This will start up the node console. Now, let's execute some `web3` commands. First, let's import `web3` and set its provider. If you recall, we did the same thing in the previous chapter. Inside the node terminal, run the following commands to import `web3`:

```
var Web3 = require('web3');
var web3 = new Web3();
```

Then, set the `web3` provider to be `localhost:8545`.

```
web3 = new Web3(new Web3.providers.HttpProvider("http://localhost:8545"));
```

To get all accounts that you have in your local test network, run the following command:

```
web3.eth.getAccounts().then(console.log)
```

Notice how this version of `web3` is promise-based. This is because it's our own `web3`, which we installed in the previous chapter. We are directly accessing `web3` through the node terminal, rather than Geth's built-in JavaScript console. The `web3` in Geth's JavaScript is of a version that does support promises (as at this time).

You should see a similar output to this in your terminal:

```
Promise { <pending> }
> [ '0xf54b8CCCdE4d31149eE537263A1db74d3491fDAB',
    '0x585a25b3aeA6070BD54cf7a41295389857b5A77E',
    '0xAba74ffdc21FCbf6ab9eF01430C2e3A96682B5DC',
    '0xCB54122C72d897C06EeBD3A0F57437A838f2cEf4',
    '0x07151274f09F3BCeb1267672f4E7aAF363882F73',
    '0x639B6Dc466129b0e194892493948A03a23741A00',
    '0xEB9bFAaF1A9FFB95829c2B8247B8843b56b820C9',
    '0xBA098ff569b884aCD8ad55CaDef00a578A28e8e3',
    '0x345c38cead231A62053Ec5608C2f130cba286A0D',
    '0x33CB07Aef13711737DDbe738095B55D53032a583' ]
```

Notice the `Promise { <pending> }`. We are waiting for the promise to resolve. Once it resolves, we see the array of our accounts.

Choosing an Ethereum Client for Your Dapp

Let's get our coinbase. Run the following command:

```
web3.eth.getCoinbase().then(console.log)
```

This should give you something similar to this:

```
Promise { <pending> }
> 0xf54b8cccde4d31149ee537263a1db74d3491fdab
```

To get the balance of your coinbase, run the following command after you replace the address with your own coinbase address:

```
web3.eth.getBalance('0xf54b8CCCdE4d31149eE537263A1db74d3491fDAB').then(console.log)
```

You should see the following:

```
Promise { <pending> }
> 100000000000000000000
```

Why is our balance `100000000000000000000`? This is because we are inside a test blockchain, not the real one, unlike in the `geth` and `parity` environments. Inside of the `ganache-cli` environment, your coinbase comes with `100000000000000000000` wei for you to play with.

To exit the `ganache-cli` console, simply run `exit`.

So, that's `ganache` in a nutshell! In this section we:

- Connected to the main Ethereum network
- Displayed our accounts
- Displayed our coinbase
- Displayed the balance of our coinbase
- Exited the `parity` console

Now, let's briefly cover how to choose the appropriate Ethereum client for your decentralized application.

Choosing the correct Ethereum client

As you may have guessed by now, `ganache-cli` is perfect for testing your Dapp locally. It allows you to connect a test blockchain network quickly, and it gives you several accounts with pre-loaded `wei` balances. However, when you want to test your blockchain with a more realistic network, that's when `geth` and `parity` come in.

`geth` and `parity` allow you to test your decentralized application on test Ethereum networks such as Ropsten and Rinkeby. The characteristics of these networks are much more similar to the main Ethereum network than the local network when using `ganache-cli`. So, the formula is simple. For quick, local testing, use `ganache-cli`.

For testing on a realistic (or real) network, `geth`, `parity`, or another fully fledged Ethereum client will do. You can find other fully fledged Ethereum clients here: `https://ethereum.stackexchange.com/questions/269/what-exactly-is-an-ethereum-client-and-what-clients-are-there?utm_medium=organicutm_source=google_rich_qautm_campaign=google_rich_qa`.

Now, let's look at how these Ethereum clients interact with Truffle.

Truffle and Ethereum clients

Before we see how Truffle integrates with Geth, Parity, and Ganache, we need to create the folder where we will place the code for this chapter:

1. Inside the `truffle-practice` folder, create a new folder called `chapter3`.
2. Copy all the contents of `chapter1` to `chapter3`.
3. Ensure that `chapter3` works without errors by performing the **Build Steps**.
4. Inside `chapter3\truffle.js` in `chapter3`, change the port property of the `module.exports.networks.development` object to `8545`. This will tell Truffle to correctly point to our local blockchain.

Your final `truffle.js` file should look like this:

```
// Allows us to use ES6 in our migrations and tests.
require('babel-register')

module.exports = {
  networks: {
    development: {
      host: '127.0.0.1',
```

```
        port: 8545,
        network_id: '*' // Match any network id
    }
  }
}
```

Now, we're ready to see how Truffle works with Geth, Parity, and Ganache-CLI.

Don't worry about which network we connect to for the following sections. We are simply seeing how Truffle interacts with Geth and Parity. In the next chapter, we will deploy our contracts to Ethereum test networks such as Ropsten and Parity.

Truffle and Geth

First, let's make sure `geth` is running. In a terminal window, run the following command:

`geth --rpc --verbosity "0" console`

The `--rpc` flag tells `geth` to connect to a locally running Ethereum node at `localhost:8545`.

Once you are in the `geth` console, make sure to unlock your coinbase account. Why must we do this? To perform transactions (a migration is a transaction, too) we need to have an unlocked coinbase account. To unlock your account, run the following command:

`web3.personal.unlockAccount(web3.eth.coinbase, "<your password>", 15000)`

Replace `<your password>` with your coinbase password. The `15000` parameter tells `geth` to keep your account unlocked for `15000` seconds.

Write this down somewhere! You may need to frequently unlock your account, and it helps if you have it nearby.

This way, you can avoid searching for it every time.

Now, in another tab, you can run the following commands to compile and migrate your Truffle contract, inside the `chapter3` folder:

`rm -rf build`
`truffle compile`
`truffle migrate`

You can see how a migration is attempted, but you may possibly receive an error. Don't worry if you do; we will cover this in the next chapter. The point is, Truffle picked up the local `geth` blockchain and attempted a migration. How do we know Truffle picked it up? We know this because we when we try to migrate, we don't see the following error:

```
Could not connect to your Ethereum client. Please check that your Ethereum
client:
 - is running
 - is accepting RPC connections (i.e., "--rpc" option is used in geth)
 - is accessible over the network
 - is properly configured in your Truffle configuration file (truffle.js)
```

If you see this error, it means that Truffle has not even recognized your Ethereum client. So, if you don't see it, that's good news!

You will learn how to *successfully* (without errors) migrate your contracts to various Ethereum networks in the next chapter.

Now, let's get Truffle to recognize `parity`.

Truffle and Parity

First, let's make sure `parity` is running. In a terminal window, run the following command:

```
parity --geth
```

Run `geth attach` in another console, and unlock your coinbase account, as usual.

```
web3.personal.unlockAccount(web3.eth.coinbase, "<your password>", 15000)
```

Replace `<your password>` with your coinbase password. The `15000` parameter tells `geth` to keep your account unlocked for `15000` seconds.

Now, in another tab, you can run the following commands to compile and migrate your Truffle contract, inside of the `chapter3` folder:

```
rm -rf build
truffle compile
truffle migrate
```

You can see how a migration is attempted, but you may possibly receive an error. Don't worry if you do; we will cover this in the next chapter. The point is, Truffle picked up the local `parity` blockchain and attempted a migration. How do we know Truffle picked it up? We know this because we when we try to migrate, we don't see the following error:

```
Could not connect to your Ethereum client. Please check that your Ethereum
client:
 - is running
 - is accepting RPC connections (i.e., "--rpc" option is used in geth)
 - is accessible over the network
 - is properly configured in your Truffle configuration file (truffle.js)
```

If you see this error, it means that Truffle has not even recognized your Ethereum client. So, if you don't see it, once again, that is good news.
You will learn how to *successfully* (without errors) migrate your contracts to various Ethereum networks in the next chapter.

Now, let's see how Truffle works with `ganache-cli`.

Truffle and Ganache-CLI

First, let's make sure `ganache-cli` is running. In a terminal window, run the following command:

`ganache-cli`

Now, in another tab, you can run the following commands to compile and migrate your Truffle contract, inside of the `chapter3` folder:

```
rm -rf build
truffle compile
truffle migrate
```

You should see a successful migration. What we did is very similar to what we did in Build Steps. The only difference is that, before, we used `truffle develop` and typed `compile` and `migrate` directly into the Truffle console. This is the preferred way to have Truffle interact with `ganache-cli`, but I just wanted to show you how to get Truffle to interact with `ganache-cli` using an alternative method, similar to what we did for the `geth` and `parity` sections before.

Summary

There was not a lot of coding in this chapter, but we covered a vital aspect of building decentralized applications. Knowing the different Ethereum clients out there and how to use them will support you when you build more Dapps.

Remember, an Ethereum client is just software that has implemented the Ethereum protocol, which allows it to gain access to a network, post transactions, mine, and more. It allows you to be the node on the blockchain network.

The next chapter will be more fun; we will learn how to successfully migrate your app to Ethereum networks of your choice.

4
Migrating Your Dapp to Ethereum Blockchains

This chapter will teach you how to correctly migrate your Truffle application to Ethereum blockchains. You will learn that migrating your application is a fundamental component in creating a fully shippable, decentralized application. Moreover, you will learn about and work with Ethereum test networks such as Ropsten and Kovan. Lastly, you will learn and uncover common pitfalls when attempting to migrate your application.

Specifically, you will:

- Learn and understand how to migrate and deploy a Truffle contract
- Learn and understand how to configure Truffle to deploy to the appropriate network
- Learn and understand common migration pitfalls and how to mitigate them

Technical requirements

You will be required to have basic knowledge of JavaScript and web development as well as Ethereum/blockchain. Finally, to use the Git repository of this book, the user needs to install Git.

The code files of this chapter can be found on GitHub:
`https://github.com/PacktPublishing/Truffle-Quick-Start-Guide/tree/master/Chapter04`

Check out the following video to see the code in action:
`http://bit.ly/2IfW60e`

Let's migrate

As mentioned in the previous chapter, we can migrate our smart contracts to various Ethereum blockchains using Geth. So, let's cover how to migrate to various Ethereum networks with Parity.

Firstly, what does it even mean to `migrate` a contract? Migrating simply means putting your contract on a specific Ethereum network so that it is accessible to and usable by others, be it other humans or computers.

You will often see the word *deploy* being used instead of *migrate*. In the context of smart contracts and decentralized applications, and Ethereum, just know that the words *deploy* and *migrate* are interchangeable.

First, let's do some housekeeping to prepare for the work we will be doing in this chapter:

1. Create a new folder called `chapter4`.
2. Copy all of the contents from `chapter3` into `chapter4`.
3. Perform the Build Steps to ensure that the project runs and works as expected (it should be no different to the projects in the first, second, and third chapters):
    - `cd chapter4`
    - `rm -rf build`
    - `truffle develop`
    - `compile`
    - `migrate`
    - `npm run dev` in another terminal window
    - Head over to `http://localhost:8080/`

Your screen should look like this, and perform correctly, as usual:

Chapter 4

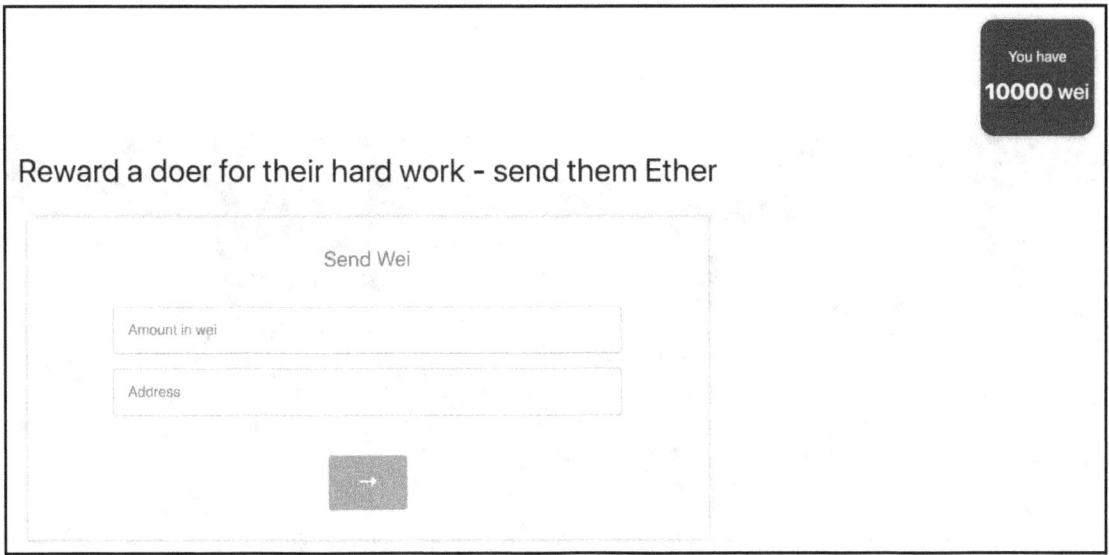

Great. Now we are all set to start migrating. Let's see how this is done with Parity.

Migrating your contracts to Ropsten with Parity

Ropsten is one of the various test Ethereum networks. It closely resembles the main network in terms of its transaction and mining structures. The difference is, of course, that none of the transactions or `ether` transferred in the Ropsten network are real. Think of Ropsten as a test environment.

When trying to ship to Ropsten, you are required to sync with the current state of the Ropsten blockchain. Unfortunately, this takes a long time with Geth. However, with Parity, we can achieve the same thing as part of a quicker and easier process.

Why not just use `ganache-cli` to test? `ganache-cli` is simply a framework to quickly and locally test your contract on a locally generated blockchain. It is not designed to resemble realistic Ethereum networks, so it should *not* be the *only* environment you should use as a test before migrating your contract to the main Ethereum network.

Let's execute some familiar steps to get a `parity` environment up and running. In a new Terminal window, run the following command:

```
parity --geth --chain ropsten
```

Migrating Your Dapp to Ethereum Blockchains

We specify `--chain ropsten` to connect to Ropsten.

The above `parity` command should give us a Terminal screen similar to this:

```
2018-04-23 14:39:09  Starting Parity/v1.8.11-stable-21522ff-20180227/x86_64-macos/rustc1.24.0
2018-04-23 14:39:09  Keys path /Users/nikhilwins/Library/Application Support/io.parity.ethereum/keys/Ropsten
2018-04-23 14:39:09  DB path /Users/nikhilwins/Library/Application Support/io.parity.ethereum/chains/test/db/ae90623718e47d66
2018-04-23 14:39:09  Path to dapps /Users/nikhilwins/Library/Application Support/io.parity.ethereum/dapps
2018-04-23 14:39:09  State DB configuration: fast
2018-04-23 14:39:09  Operating mode: active
2018-04-23 14:39:09  Configured for Ropsten using Ethash engine
2018-04-23 14:39:11  Updated conversion rate to Ξ1 = US$639.50 (186157330 wei/gas)
2018-04-23 14:39:15  Public node URL: enode://9b6f165951d72ed1a592f37af85c9a24a68ad6a4b3844028bcda397c24f8348b5dbfc86568b0733896306c707a68836b59d8279ef92f7464dbdd066db
b6942b5@10.100.0.238:30303
2018-04-23 14:39:20  Syncing #3073619 bc4a_f022    1 blk/s  108 tx/s    3 Mgas/s     68+  127 Qed  #3073833  10/25 peers   352 KiB chain 65 MiB db  12 MiB queue  3 MiB
sync  RPC:  0 conn,  0 req/s,   0 µs
2018-04-23 14:39:30  Syncing #3073758 374e_58fd   13 blk/s 1178 tx/s   47 Mgas/s      0+  483 Qed  #3074243  10/25 peers    2 MiB chain 69 MiB db  30 MiB queue 31 MiB s
ync   RPC:  0 conn,  0 req/s,   0 µs
2018-04-23 14:39:40  Syncing #3074045 6539_4871   28 blk/s 1821 tx/s   73 Mgas/s   2998+ 1217 Qed  #3078716  10/25 peers    6 MiB chain 73 MiB db 128 MiB queue 12 MiB
sync  RPC:  0 conn,  0 req/s,   0 µs
2018-04-23 14:39:50  Syncing #3074333 c294_ccc6   29 blk/s 2217 tx/s   86 Mgas/s    457+ 3893 Qed  #3078716  10/25 peers    6 MiB chain 76 MiB db 220 MiB queue 12 MiB
sync  RPC:  0 conn,  0 req/s,   0 µs
2018-04-23 14:40:00  Syncing #3074855 26f9_581e   52 blk/s 2913 tx/s  118 Mgas/s      0+ 3860 Qed  #3078716  11/25 peers    6 MiB chain 78 MiB db 207 MiB queue 12 MiB
sync  RPC:  0 conn,  0 req/s,   0 µs
2018-04-23 14:40:10  Syncing #3075529 9f50_7cac   67 blk/s 3899 tx/s  157 Mgas/s      0+ 3184 Qed  #3078716  11/25 peers    6 MiB chain 79 MiB db 171 MiB queue 12 MiB
sync  RPC:  0 conn,  0 req/s,   0 µs
2018-04-23 14:40:20  Syncing #3076263 b9d3_e8ae   73 blk/s 4346 tx/s  143 Mgas/s      0+ 2452 Qed  #3078716  11/25 peers    6 MiB chain 79 MiB db 133 MiB queue 12 MiB
sync  RPC:  0 conn,  0 req/s,   0 µs
2018-04-23 14:40:25  Syncing #3076641 a3ea_94fa   75 blk/s 4572 tx/s  129 Mgas/s      0+ 2072 Qed  #3078716  11/25 peers    6 MiB chain 79 MiB db 114 MiB queue 12 MiB
sync  RPC:  0 conn,  0 req/s,   0 µs
2018-04-23 14:40:35  Syncing #3077227 7588_0a8a   58 blk/s 3826 tx/s  117 Mgas/s      0+ 1488 Qed  #3078716  11/25 peers    6 MiB chain 80 MiB db  81 MiB queue 12 MiB s
ync.  RPC:  0 conn,  0 req/s,   0 µs
2018-04-23 14:40:40  Syncing #3077596 ec22_78b7   73 blk/s 4947 tx/s  155 Mgas/s      0+ 1116 Qed  #3078716  11/25 peers    6 MiB chain 81 MiB db  59 MiB queue 12 MiB s
```

I highlighted `Configured for Ropsten using Ethash engine`. Clearly, we have connected to the Ropsten network.

To use the the JavaScript console, in another Terminal window or tab, run the following command:

`geth attach`

After running the previous commands, we should see a screen, in the other Terminal window, that looks similar to this:

```
Welcome to the Geth JavaScript console!

instance: Geth/v1.8.2-stable/darwin-amd64/go1.10
coinbase: 0xd35db5027107f222566894caaf987e9051269ece
at block: 0 (Thu, 01 Jan 1970 07:00:00 +07)
 modules: eth:1.0 net:1.0 personal:1.0 rpc:1.0 web3:1.0

>
```

Chapter 4

Great. Now that you're connected to Ropsten, try to perform a `truffle migrate`, that is, in another Terminal tab (the third tab, I know!):

```
cd chapter4
rm -rf build
truffle compile
truffle migrate
```

You should see the following error:

```
Could not connect to your Ethereum client. Please check that your Ethereum
client:
 - is running
 - is accepting RPC connections (i.e., "--rpc" option is used in geth)
 - is accessible over the network
 - is properly configured in your Truffle configuration file (truffle.js)
```

Can you guess what's missing?

The answer lies in the `truffle.js` file at the root level of your project:

```
// Allows us to use ES6 in our migrations and tests.
require('babel-register')

module.exports = {
  networks: {
    development: {
      host: '127.0.0.1',
      port: 8545,
      network_id: '*' // Match any network id
    }
  }
}
```

There is no indication of the Ropsten network. It's not in the `networks` object. We need to tell Truffle that we plan to deploy our contracts to Ropsten. So, inside of the `networks` object, add the following code:

```
      ropsten: {
        network_id: 3,
        host: "127.0.0.1",
        port: 8545,
        gas: 2900000
      }
```

[73]

Migrating Your Dapp to Ethereum Blockchains

The Ropsten network ID is 3, as you can see. The host is the same, and we specify a large gas amount. You will learn later in this chapter, that migrating a contract to any network costs gas. Of course, migrating your contract to a test network like Ropsten does not consume real gas, but nonetheless, you can specify a maximum gas amount that you are willing to have consumed when you deploy the contract.

The minimum block gas amount is 21000, but as you can see, we specify an amount significantly above that. You will learn how to play with the gas amount later in this chapter. For now, we are specifying a large gas amount to be on the safe side. This does not mean that all of the 2900000 gas will be consumed. It simply acts as an upper bound of the gas we are *willing* to spend for the migration.

Your final `truffle.js` file should look like this:

```
// Allows us to use ES6 in our migrations and tests.
require('babel-register')

module.exports = {
  networks: {
    development: {
      host: '127.0.0.1',
      port: 8545,
      network_id: '*' // Match any network id
    },
    ropsten: {
      network_id: 3,
      host: "127.0.0.1",
      port: 8545,
      gas: 4612388
    }
  }
}
```

You'll notice that we set a gas of 4612388. Why? Well, it was a result of experimentation. As we've briefly covered before, the gas you send along with your transaction is essentially the fuel or reward needed by the miners to validate and process your transaction. The real gas used up is obviously determined by your code, but you can also manually and liberally specify an amount of gas that you think will be sufficient for your transaction to get processed.

We will cover more about gas, gas price, and gas limits in our final chapter.

Let's migrate to Ropsten now. First, make sure your `parity` console is still running. Then, in another Terminal window, run the following command:

```
truffle migrate --network ropsten
```

Notice how we specify the name of our network along with the `--network` flag. We do this because simply running `truffle migrate` defaults to the development network, as seen in the earlier chapters.

Truffle knows what `ropsten` is because we specified this in the `networks` object in our `truffle.js` file.

When you run `truffle migrate --network ropsten`, you *may* still see an error:

```
Expected parameter 'from' not passed to function.
```

We will get this error if we have no accounts in our Ropsten network. You can confirm this by the following command in your `parity` JavaScript console:

```
web3.eth.accounts
```

If you have no Ropsten accounts, you should see the following:

```
[]
```

Accordingly, we need to find a way to create accounts in Ropsten. If you already have an account, you can skip the preceding section and move to the *Syncing Parity to Ropsten* section.

Creating a new Ropsten Parity account

If you already have Ropsten accounts in Geth, you can simply import them to Parity. Quit the process running Parity, and run the following command:

```
parity --import-geth-keys --chain ropsten
```

Once again, we specify `--chain ropsten` to ensure that we are importing Geth keys from Ropsten.

If you don't have Ropsten accounts in `geth`, you can simply create a new Ropsten account for Parity under the Parity UI.

Migrating Your Dapp to Ethereum Blockchains

You can do this by executing the following command first:

```
parity --chain ropsten ui
```

This should open a new tab in your browser that looks something like this:

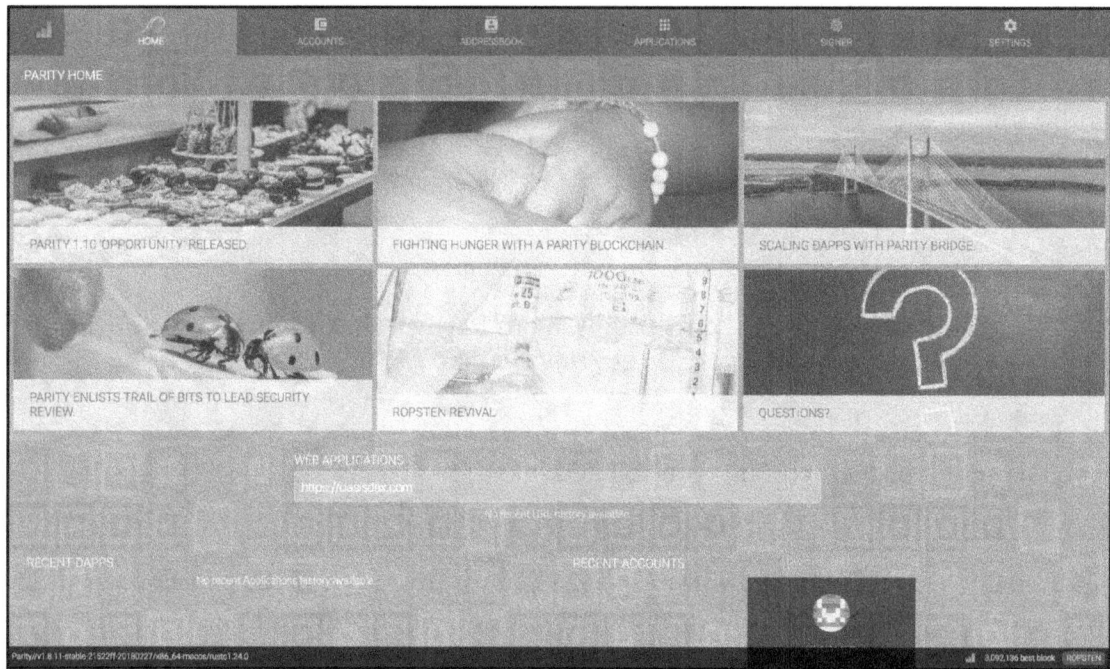

To create a new account, click on the **Accounts** tab, then click **New Account**. Follow the instructions.

Now, let's start up the `parity` node with our commands again:

```
parity --geth --chain ropsten
```

Once again, in another Terminal, open a JavaScript console by running the following command:

```
geth attach
```

To confirm that we indeed have an account in our Ropsten network in Parity, run the following command to get all accounts:

```
web3.eth.coinbase
```

You should now see a coinbase account, similar to this:

```
> web3.eth.coinbase
"0xb1fa39f962682f8c85cdf1e21042712195a74b14"
>
```

If you don't, it's probably because your node has not been synced fully yet. Let's see how to sync our Parity node to the current state of the Ropsten blockchain.

Syncing Parity to Ropsten

You can check the sync status by running the following command inside the JavaScript console while your Parity node is still running:

```
web3.eth.syncing
```

If your node has not fully synced yet, you will see a JavaScript object output to the console, similar to this:

```
> web3.eth.syncing
{
    currentBlock: 3099084,
    highestBlock: 3099092,
    startingBlock: 3095513,
    warpChunksAmount: null,
    warpChunksProcessed: null
}
```

As you can see, our current block is less than the highest block, meaning we still have a few more blocks to download before we are fully synced with Ropsten.

If you are fully synced, you will see the following response in your console:

If you find that your node is taking too long to sync, you can increase the cache size to quicken the processing time of blocks by specifying the `--cache-size` flag.

If you would like more information on how exactly to use this flag, check out this helpful resource: https://ethereum.stackexchange.com/questions/10465/is-it-possible-to-make-the-parity-software-sync-faster.

Now, in order for us to be able to perform any transaction using our coinbase, we need to have a positive balance of `ether` in our coinbase account. As a reminder, you can get the balance of your coinbase account by running the following command:

```
web3.eth.getBalance(web3.eth.coinbase);
```

If you have a balance of at least one `ether` in your account already, you can skip the next section and move straight to the *Migrating our contract to Ropsten* Section.

Adding funds to our Parity coinbase account

You can add `ether` to your coinbase balance in a few ways; the quickest and easiest way is to start mining. Unlike in Geth, mining in Parity is not as simple as adding a `--mine` flag. In short, you need to find a module called `ethminer` and use it in combination with Parity to mine. We will not cover this in detail here, but you can find a full instructions list here: https://wiki.parity.io/Mining.

Another common way is to use MetaMask. We've mentioned this briefly in Chapter 1, *Truffle for Decentralized Applications*, but we have not really delved into what exactly MetaMask is.

As you develop more decentralized applications, you will come across MetaMask more often. What is MetaMask? MetaMask is simply a tool that allows you to connect with various Ethereum networks. You'll see what I mean when we head over to the following link to install MetaMask: `https://metamask.io/`.

MetaMask is a Chrome extension. Once you install it, you will need to set up a few housekeeping things, including a username and a password. Once you set it up, you can log in, and see that you can connect to various Ethereum networks:

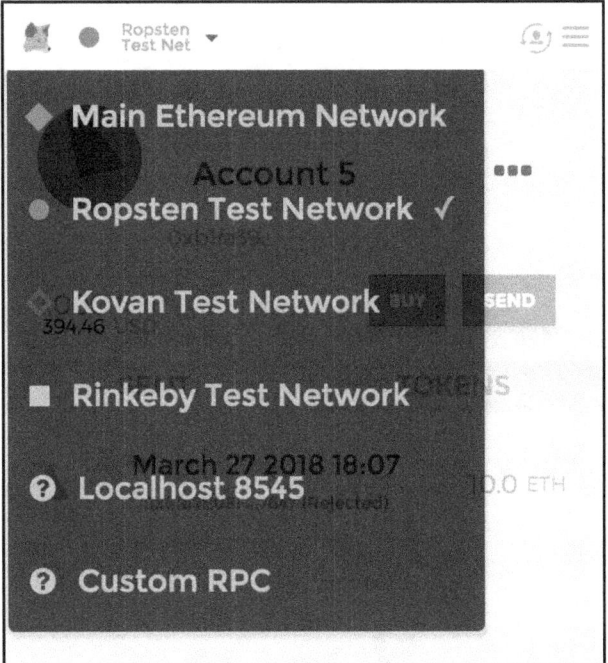

 This is not meant to be a comprehensive tutorial on MetaMask, so please use the following resources if you need more information; the goal is to simply load `ether` into our account, and MetaMask is merely one of the ways to do it.

If you are connected to Ropsten on Parity on `localhost:8545`, you can connect to **Localhost 8545** with MetaMask. To transfer `ether` to your account, you can use a faucet. A faucet is just a tool that holds a bunch of `ether`, which you can tap to get `ether`. Test `ether`, obviously. You can find a Ropsten faucet here: `https://faucet.metamask.io/`.

Once you get there, just request some `ether` from the faucet:

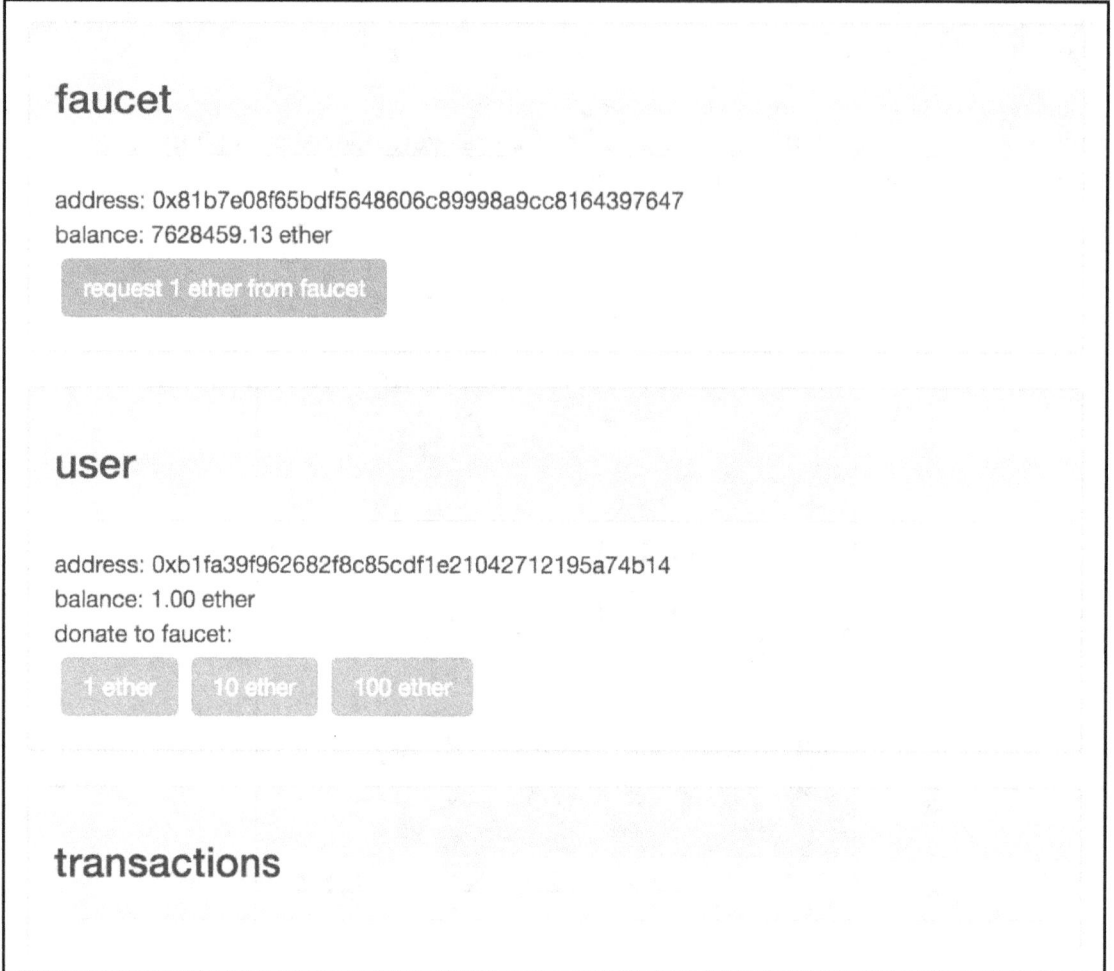

Migrating our contract to Ropsten

Okay, we finally have some `ether` in our coinbase account! Now, let's migrate. Let's do a quick check to make sure we are ready:

- `parity` is running
- Our `coinbase` account is unlocked
- Our `coinbase` has a positive `ether` balance

But wait, how do we unlock our coinbase account in Parity? It's a little different from Geth. You can start with your account unlocked by starting the Parity node in the following way:

```
parity --geth --chain ropsten --unlock
0xb1fa39f962682f8c85cdf1e21042712195a74b14 --password password.txt
```

Let's look at the new flags we are using:

- We use the `--unlock` flag and pass our coinbase account. Yours will be different.
- We use the `--password` flag and pass a file containing our password in raw text.

So, create a file in the root level of your project called `password.txt`, and dump your password in there, at the top, with nothing more. You should not do this in production, but since we are simply testing on Ropsten, this will suffice. In the final chapter *Truffle Gotchas and Best Practices*, you will learn the best practices of Truffle, smart contract, and dapp development.

Great! Now, when you run the following command, you should start Parity with your coinbase account unlocked. Remember, for this to work, you need to be inside the `chapter4` folder when you run your terminal commands.

Now, we are free to perform transactions, so let's migrate our contract!

To migrate, run the following command:

```
truffle migrate --network ropsten
```

Now, you should see a successful migration.

```
Running migration: 1_initial_migration.js
  Deploying Migrations...
  ... 0xb390aff820e20a984c1360b0caed0f5ee48709d0bbe35c4859d9e07df056ad31
  Migrations: 0xddcdca6ab896af6bf35eaf8845a4d66aea1ef836
Saving successful migration to network...
  ... 0x24f91429894a2a5859a01cb17ebb7a467311ba807fbb4fc9522063ee8565b7a5
Saving artifacts...
Running migration: 2_deploy_contracts.js
  Deploying TaskMaster...
  ... 0x03f3ec36aeabaa1fa88a8d6473c56b1495aa53cb86e637cebd30c218f73b9180
  TaskMaster: 0x5ebb1d96fb1046c339c9719f186fb33f9894c74f
Saving successful migration to network...
  ... 0xb8c49c03b2e8fb50c32c3ca8fe7678ce9c5778a889513cf27ff2c329d45f621a
Saving artifacts...
```

Great! We've seen how to connect and deploy to Ropsten using `parity` as our Ethereum client. How about if we wanted to migrate our contract to another Ethereum network, say, Kovan?

Migrating our contract to kovan

Let's go back to our `truffle.js` configuration file. In the same way we added an entry for Ropsten, we simply have to add another entry to the networks object for Kovan.

```
kovan: {
  host: "127.0.0.1",
  port: 8545,
  network_id: 42,
  gas: 4612388
}
```

Notice the network ID of `42`. This is the network ID for Kovan.

Then, we simply switch `parity` to connect to Kovan.

```
parity --geth --chain kovan --unlock
0xb1fa39f962682f8c85cdf1e21042712195a74b14 --password password.txt
```

As usual, perform a Truffle migration.

```
truffle migrate --network kovan
```

You should see a successful migration again:

```
Running migration: 1_initial_migration.js
  Replacing Migrations...
  ... 0xb95007417a6d7182d43fb4de9e70d0422c2b8daf6d6d946d12874b1cf0c1c996
  Migrations: 0xc8c9d0bd9f56868fa186460bb602e7854de40d8a
Saving successful migration to network...
  ... 0x0c212d03301f9619854cfb24a71def9d26c1d03feaaebd021525ecaca84e5149
Saving artifacts...
Running migration: 2_deploy_contracts.js
  Replacing TaskMaster...
  ... 0xfa4ecfd1ccdb2eda8a7068bc7b9927b2e0ee0e454514c3168cf6d3477df46f43
  TaskMaster: 0xfe0d504eef2507b11f2eb84869f9182221dc01a4
Saving artifacts...
```

 You may notice some of the same errors you encountered when trying to deploy to Ropsten. Follow the same troubleshooting steps we went through to resolve the issue.

What if we want to deploy our contract to the main Ethereum network? In order to deploy to the main network, you will need real `ether` to deploy your contract. I suggest you don't do this unless you are making a real smart contract to be served and used. If you want to just test, that's what networks like Ropsten and Kovan are for. They closely resemble the main network, so deploying to Ropsten and Kovan and getting the hang of that should prepare you well for when you decide to migrate your contract to the main network.

You've seen how to migrate your contract to various networks. What's left? Well, we didn't do this without encountering a few errors along the way. So, what are some of the common challenges you encounter when trying to migrate your contract?

Common migration pitfalls

A common mistake is to have a misconfigured `truffle.js` file. Ensure that for each network you plan to deploy to, there should be a corresponding entry in the `networks` object, stating the following information:

```
networks: {
  network_name: {
    network_id: <number>
    host: <string>,
    port: <number>,
    gas: <number>
  }
}
```

How do we know what is the correct gas limit? Well, you have to play with this a little.

Every transaction you make has a gas cost. A migration is a transaction, too, and thus has a gas cost. When attemmpting to migrate your contract, you may run into this error:

```
exceeds block gas limit
```

Every transaction you send has a gas limit. Try to decrease the amount of gas specified.

Another error you may encounter is the following:

```
insufficient funds for gas * price + value
```

This means the total cost of the transaction exceeds your account's balance. So, you need to add more `ether` to your account.

You may see the following error when trying to perform a Truffle migration:

```
Expected parameter 'from' not passed to function
```

This means that you don't have any accounts in the network you are trying to deploy to. So, make sure you add at least one account.

Lastly, you may receive the following error:

```
Intrinsic gas too low
```

Every transaction costs a minimum of `21000` gas. If you see this error, you need to allocate more gas to your transaction.

> For other errors, you can post a question on the Ethereum Stack Exchange here: `https://ethereum.stackexchange.com/`, or on the Ethereum subreddit here: `https://www.reddit.com/r/ethereum/`.
>
> People post questions on these websites periodically, and they are there to help you. Remember, many of your questions, bugs, or problems may already have been faced and fixed by someone. Ask for help!

> When using `geth`, make sure your account is unlocked.
>
> Your account will be locked unless you specify for it to be unlocked for a long period of time.

Summary

We learned how to migrate your contract using `geth` to Ropsten and Kovan, and the principles we learned will allow us to migrate on to the main Ethereum network when we are ready to deploy a real-world contract.

Once again, we use `parity` and `geth` because they can connect to real Ethereum networks such as Ropsten and Kovan, unlike `ganache-cli`.

I will see you in the next chapter, where we will learn to how integrate our Truffle project with some of the most popular JavaScript frameworks, such as Angular, React, and Vue.

5
Truffle and Popular JavaScript Technologies

This chapter will illustrate the use of Truffle with modern JavaScript technologies such as Angular, React, and Node. You will learn how to integrate Truffle with JavaScript frontend libraries and frameworks as well as on the backend with Node. This chapter will provide code snippets and examples for various frameworks, and highlight the integration similarities between all frameworks. Moreover, this chapter will cover the best practices that you can employ when integrating Truffle with a modern JavaScript framework, library, or technology.

More specifically, you will learn the following:

- How to integrate Truffle with Angular
- How to integrate Truffle with React
- How to integrate Truffle with Node

Up until now, we worked with Truffle without using a JavaScript frontend framework. We did this to focus on Truffle and learn how it works to combine web3, JavaScript, and Solidity, and not to allow complex JavaScript frameworks to distract us. However, it is crucial to work with a modern, robust, and scalable JavaScript framework when writing a real-world, decentralized application.

What are some of the most common JavaScript frameworks or libraries? The most used JavaScript technologies on the frontend are Angular and React. As for the backend, well, Node is the most commonly used runtime that enables us to write JavaScript server-side. So, in this chapter, you will learn how to integrate Truffle with Angular, React, and Node. We'll start with the frontend first, and in particular, Angular.

 It is **not** necessary to complete this chapter in order. If you are not interested in Angular but only in React, say, you can skip to the *Truffle and React* section.

Technical requirements

You will be required to have basic knowledge of JavaScript and web development as well as Ethereum/blockchain. Finally, to use the Git repository of this book, the user needs to install Git.

The code files for this chapter can be found on GitHub:
`https://github.com/PacktPublishing/Truffle-Quick-Start-Guide/tree/master/Chapter05`

Check out the following video to see the code in action:
`http://bit.ly/2K8mA8K`

Truffle and Angular

Let's build a small Dapp using Truffle and Angular 4/5.

 This is not meant to be a tutorial on the inner workings of Angular. If you are not familiar with Angular, I suggest you read up on it first; here is a good place to start: `https://angular.io/tutorial`.

Once you have a basic understanding of Angular, you are ready to begin this section.

Let's get started.

Like any good app, we need a robust and maintainable boilerplate before we start writing code. I've already set one up. Let's dive into the boilerplate.

angular-truffle-starter-dapp

You can find `angular-truffle-starter-dapp` here: https://github.com/PacktPublishing/Truffle-Quick-Start-Guide/tree/master/chapter5/truffle-angular. At the time of writing this book, `angular-truffle-starter-dapp` is the most used Angular and Truffle integration, with currently over 150 stars and 60 forks on GitHub.

Before we begin using this starter, we must ensure we have a folder to work out of. As usual, let's create some folders to begin working on this chapter.

Inside our `truffle-practice` folder, perform the following:

1. Create a new folder called `chapter5`
2. Go into `chapter5` (`cd chapter5`)
3. Create a new folder called `truffle-angular`
4. Head over to the link mentioned above for the Angular-Truffle starter
5. Clone it inside the `truffle-angular` folder

Your `truffle-angular` folder structure should look like this—the important folders and files are **bolded**:

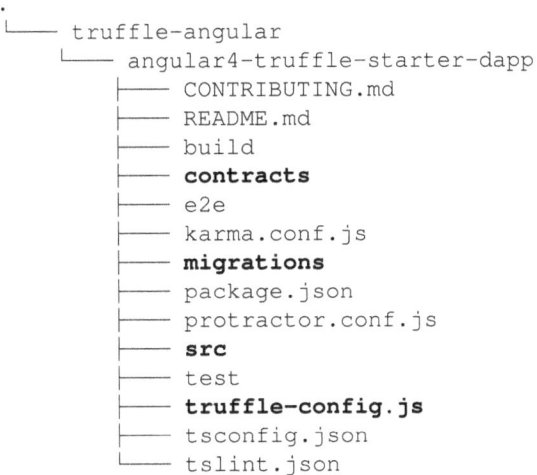

The `contracts` and `migrations` folders are there as usual—you should already be familiar with them. The `truffle-config.js` is where our networks are defined—have a look inside—but again, you should already be familiar with this.

One folder you may be unfamiliar with is the `src` folder. Let's take a look inside to learn and understand its structure.

Peeping into the src folder

The `src` folder structure should look something like this. I've highlighted the important folders in **bold**:

```
├── app
│   ├── app.component.html
│   ├── app.component.spec.ts
│   ├── app.component.ts
│   └── app.module.ts
├── assets
│   ├── demo.gif
│   └── logo.png
├── environments
│   ├── environment.prod.ts
│   └── environment.ts
├── favicon.ico
├── index.html
├── main.ts
├── polyfills.ts
├── services
│   ├── meta-coin.service.spec.ts
│   ├── meta-coin.service.ts
│   ├── services.ts
│   ├── web3.service.spec.ts
│   └── web3.service.ts
├── styles.css
├── test.ts
├── tsconfig.app.json
├── tsconfig.spec.json
├── typings.d.ts
└── util
    ├── validation.spec.ts
    └── validation.ts
```

The `app` folder will contain all the root UI files for our app—the HTML, CSS, and Typescript files. We'll see how this works when we run this app. For now, it is important to note that our UI and component logic is housed in `app.component.ts`.

The `services` folder is where our web3 and MetaCoin services are. What is MetaCoin?

Chapter 5

Well, if you peek into the `contracts` folder, you will see a contract called `MetaCoin.sol`. This is the main smart contract of this starter Dapp, and in fact, it's a common contract you will find in many Truffle starter apps including Truffle's own.

The `web3.service.ts` file involves instantiating `web3` and setting its provider. The `meta-coin.service.ts` files involve creating a usable JavaScript abstraction of our smart contract, which allows us to interact with its public functions. We will see all of this in more detail very soon, but once again, we have already covered these concepts in previous chapters. The only difference here is that the code is inside an Angular environment.

Before we peep into the code, let's first run this project to get a feel for how it looks.

Running the starter Dapp

The instructions here are divided into two small parts, for your convenience.

Part 1

Inside the `angular-truffle-starter-dapp` folder, install all dependencies with `npm install`.

Part 2

In another Terminal window/tab, run `ganache-cli` to start a local blockchain.

And then, in the original tab, run the following:

1. `truffle compile` to compile your contracts.
2. `truffle migrate` to deploy those contracts to the network.
3. `ng serve` to start your application.
4. Navigate to `http://localhost:4200/`. The app will automatically reload if you change any of the source files.
5. Make sure there are no errors in browser console.

You can also run `npm run compile-start` to run the first three steps automatically.

Since you have `ganache-cli` running, make sure MetaMask is switched off as this could cause problems with web3 being set correctly.

[91]

On `http://localhost:4200/`, you should see the following screen:

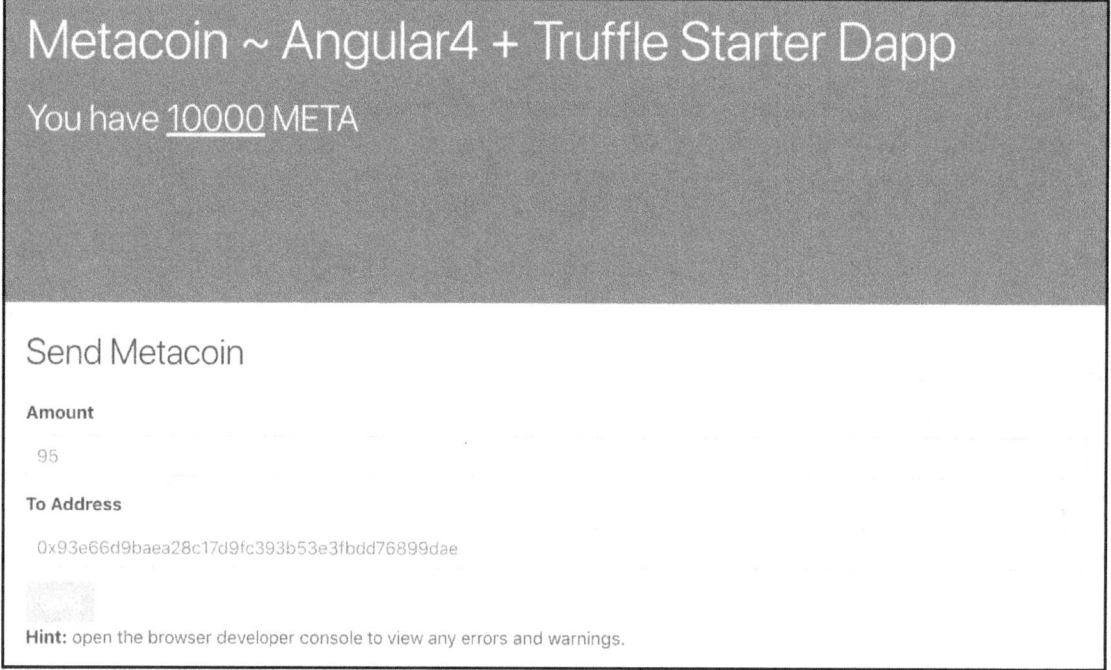

If you look in `app.html` in the `src/app` folder, you will see that this HTML file contains all of the elements you see in this UI.

Chapter 5

Let's play around really quickly. First enter a recipient address, then send a coin. I sent `50` MetaCoin to `0x85db1e131b6c5c0c7eec98fed091a441ed856424`.

Here's what my screen looks like:

When you hit the **Send** button, you should see your balance update to something like this. If you chose to send 50 MetaCoin, you should see the following:

You have 9950 META

Okay, but what controls the logic behind this screen? Let's take a look inside `app`, in particular, `app.component.ts`.

First, let's look at the constructor:

```
constructor(
  private _ngZone: NgZone,
  private web3Service: Web3Service,
  private metaCoinService: MetaCoinService,
) {
  this.onReady();
}
```

Notice how we inject instances of `Web3Service` and `MetaCoinService` into the constructor through Angular's dependency injection. If you want to learn more about the dependency injection in Angular, this resource is helpful: https://angular.io/guide/dependency-injection.

But, in short, dependency injection allows you simply to pop in the classes you want to use without worrying about manually instantiating the classes.

Notice how we include the `Web3Service` and `MetaCoinService` services at the top of the file with our other `import` statements:

```
import {Web3Service, MetaCoinService} from '../services/services'
```

Also, in the constructor, we call the `onReady` function. Let's take a look inside this function to see what is going on:

```
onReady = () => {

  // Get the initial account balance so it can be displayed.
  this.web3Service.getAccounts().subscribe(accs => {
    this.accounts = accs;
    this.account = this.accounts[0];

    // This is run from window:load and ZoneJS is not aware of it we
    // need to use _ngZone.run() so that the UI updates on promise resolution
    this._ngZone.run(() =>
```

```
        this.refreshBalance()
     );
  }, err => alert(err))
};
```

Notice how we invoke the `getAccounts` function from our `web3Service`. We'll dive into `web3Service` soon, but you can guess here that this simply gets all accounts associated with our current blockchain, *just like we've done before*—nothing new here!

We then call `refreshBalance` inside of an `NgZone`. For more information on `NgZone`, this link is helpful: https://angular.io/api/core/NgZone.

Let's take a look at what `refreshBalance` does:

```
refreshBalance = () => {
  this.metaCoinService.getBalance(this.account)
    .subscribe(value => {
      this.balance = value
    }, e => {this.setStatus('Error getting balance; see log.')})
};
```

Notice how we call the `getBalance` function of `MetaCoinService`. If you refer back to the smart contract `MetaCoin.sol` under the `contracts` folder, you can see how the public function `getBalance` of the contract is defined.

`MetaCoinService` is just a service to abstract the JavaScript object that we use to call public functions of the `MetaCoin` contract. Remember, we've done all of this before—the only difference is we are inside of an Angular environment. Conceptually, nothing is new here.

Once we get the balance using our service, we call the `setStatus` function:

```
setStatus = message => {
  this.status = message;
};
```

Pretty straightforward.

Where is the function that is hooked to the click of the **Send** button? That function is called `sendCoin`; let's take a look:

```
sendCoin = () => {
  this.setStatus('Initiating transaction... (please wait)');

  this.metaCoinService.sendCoin(this.account, this.recipientAddress,
    this.sendingAmount)
      .subscribe(() =>{
```

```
            this.setStatus('Transaction complete!');
            this.refreshBalance();
        }, e => this.setStatus('Error sending coin; see log.'))
    };
```

We call the `sendCoin` public function of `MetaCoinService`. It's getting close to the time for us to dive into `MetaCoinService`. But, before we do that, let's dive into `Web3Service`, as it is necessary to understand that before we move any further.

Under `src/services`, open the `web3.service.ts` file.

Diving into Web3Service

Firstly, notice how we include an import of `web3` at the top of the file:

```
const Web3 = require('web3');
```

Now, let's take a look at the constructor:

```
constructor() {
    this.checkAndInstantiateWeb3();
}
```

Right away, we call the `checkAndInstantiateWeb3` function. If you haven't guessed, this function checks for `web3` and instantiates it with a provider:

```
checkAndInstantiateWeb3 = () => {
    // Checking if Web3 has been injected by the browser
      (Mist/MetaMask)
    if (typeof window.web3 !== 'undefined') {
      console.warn(
        'Using web3 detected from external source. If you find that
        your accounts don\'t appear or you have 0 MetaCoin, ensure
        you\'ve configured that source properly. If using MetaMask,
        see the following link. Feel free to delete this warning. :)
        http://truffleframework.com/tutorials/truffle-and-metamask'
      );
      // Use Mist/MetaMask's provider
      this.web3 = new Web3(window.web3.currentProvider);
    } else {
      console.warn(
        'No web3 detected. Falling back to ${environment.HttpProvider}.
        You should remove this fallback when you deploy live, as it\'s
        inherently insecure. Consider switching to Metamask for
        development. More info here:
        http://truffleframework.com/tutorials/truffle-and-metamask'
```

```
    );
    // fallback - use your fallback strategy (local node / hosted
      node + in-dapp id mgmt / fail)
      this.web3 = new Web3(
        new Web3.providers.HttpProvider(environment.HttpProvider)
    );
  }
};
```

We've seen some of this before. We check if web3 is already provided by, say, MetaMask. If it is, then we make sure to use the current provider and instantiate web3 with that.

Otherwise, we fall back to the http://localhost:8080 provider of our local blockchain, as usual.

Now, let's take a look at the getAccounts function:

```
getAccounts(): Observable<any>{
  return Observable.create(observer => {
    this.web3.eth.getAccounts((err, accs) => {
      if (err != null) {
        observer.error('There was an error fetching your accounts.')
      }

      if (accs.length === 0) {
        observer.error('Couldn\'t get any accounts! Make sure your
        Ethereum client is configured correctly.')
      }

      observer.next(accs)
      observer.complete()
    });
  })
}
```

Here, we simply wrap the call of web3.eth.getAccounts inside of a function that provides the accounts in an Observable stream. This is a design preference—we could have also returned the accounts in a Promise. If you want to learn more about Observables, this resource is helpful: https://angular.io/guide/observables.

That's it with web3. Notice there there is nothing new we do with web3 or Truffle here. Once again, the only difference is that we are inside of an Angular environment, so we make the necessary *Angular* adjustments.

Let's dive into `MetaCoinService`. Under `src/services`, open the file `meta-coin.service.ts`.

MetaCoinService

The first thing you will notice is that we import `Web3Service`, `MetaCoin.json`, and `truffle-contract`. This is similar to what we did in Chapter 1, *Truffle for Decentralized Applications*, where we built a mini decentralized application:

```
import { Web3Service } from './web3.service'

const metaincoinArtifacts = require('../../build/contracts/MetaCoin.json');
const contract = require('truffle-contract');
```

Remember, `contract` allows us to have a JavaScript object where we can call public functions of this contract.

Next, we use the `metacoinartifacts` to create a usable `MetaCoin` JavaScript object. It is now an instance variable of this service:

```
MetaCoin = contract(metaincoinArtifacts);
```

Next, let's take a look at the constructor:

```
constructor(
  private web3Ser: Web3Service,
) {
  // Bootstrap the MetaCoin abstraction for Use
  this.MetaCoin.setProvider(web3Ser.web3.currentProvider);
}
```

Notice how we inject `Web3Service` through Angular's dependency injection. We use it to set a provider to `this.MetaCoin`.

Let's take a look at the first function defined, `getBalance`:

```
getBalance(account): Observable<number> {
  let meta;

  return Observable.create(observer => {
    this.MetaCoin
      .deployed()
      .then(instance => {
        meta = instance;
        //we use call here so the call doesn't try and write, making
```

```
          it free
        return meta.getBalance.call(account, {
          from: account
        });
      })
      .then(value => {
        observer.next(value)
        observer.complete()
      })
      .catch(e => {
        console.log(e);
        observer.error(e)
      });
  })
}
```

Notice how we call the `getBalance` public function of the `MetaCoin` JavaScript object. Once again, we return the balance of the account in an `Observable` stream.

Now let's take a look at the `sendCoin` function:

```
sendCoin(from, to, amount): Observable<any>{
  let meta;
  return Observable.create(observer => {
    this.MetaCoin
      .deployed()
      .then(instance => {
        meta = instance;
        return meta.sendCoin(to, amount, {
          from: from
        });
      })
      .then(() => {
        observer.next()
        observer.next()
      })
      .catch(e => {
        console.log(e);
        observer.error(e)
      });
  })
}
```

Again, we call the `sendCoin` function of MetaCoin and return the result in an `Observable` stream.

Notice how for each function on `MetaCoin`, we wrap it inside a function of `MetaCoinService`. This way, we abstract logic, and in general, it is a good programming practice.

Great! So that's just about it with Truffle and Angular. You've seen how to set up a Truffle application inside of an Angular environment. Now, let's move on to React. Close your Terminal windows so you can start a fresh.

Truffle and React

Let's build a small Dapp using Truffle and React.

This is not meant to be a tutorial on the inner workings of React. If you are not familiar with React, I suggest you read up on it first—here is a good place to start: https://reactjs.org/tutorial/tutorial.html.

Once you have a basic understanding of React, you are ready to begin this section.

Let's get started.

The Truffle and React starter

As usual, let's start with a starter. You can get the Truffle and React starter right here: https://github.com/truffle-box/react-box.

If you skipped the Angular chapter, you need to do the following first. Inside your `truffle-practice` folder, create a new folder called `chapter5`.

Now that you have a folder for this chapter, create a new folder called `truffle-react` inside the `chapter5` folder.

To set up this project, go inside `truffle-practice/chapter5/truffle-react` and run the following commands in your terminal:

1. `truffle unbox react`.
2. `truffle develop`.

Chapter 5

3. Inside the Truffle development console, run:
    - `compile`
    - `migrate`
4. Once the contracts have been successfully compiled and migrated, run `npm run start`.
5. Head over to `http://localhost:3000`.

Once you do this, on `http://localhost:3000`, you should see a screen that looks like this:

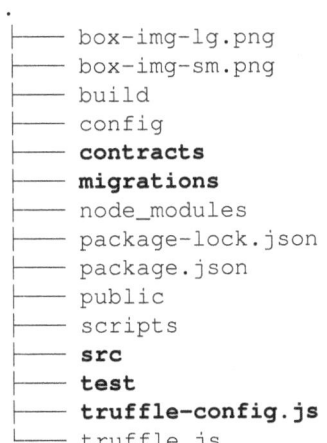

Your `truffle-react` folder structure should look like this—the important folders and files are **bolded**:

```
.
├── box-img-lg.png
├── box-img-sm.png
├── build
├── config
├── contracts
├── migrations
├── node_modules
├── package-lock.json
├── package.json
├── public
├── scripts
├── src
├── test
├── truffle-config.js
└── truffle.js
```

[101]

The `contracts` and `migrations` folders should be familiar. `truffle-config.js` is where our networks are defined—have a look inside—but again, you should already be familiar with this.

One folder you may be unfamiliar with is the `src` folder. Let's take a look inside to learn and understand its structure.

Peeping into the src folder

The `src` folder structure should look something like this. I've highlighted the important files in **bold**:

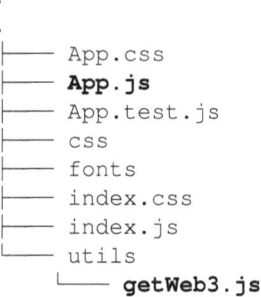

```
.
├── App.css
├── App.js
├── App.test.js
├── css
├── fonts
├── index.css
├── index.js
└── utils
    └── getWeb3.js
```

We can see the root UI files of our app—the HTML, CSS, and JavaScript files. We'll see how this works when we run this app. But, for now, it is important to note that our UI and component logic is housed in `App.js`.

The `utils` folder is where our web3 service belongs. The `getWeb3` file involves instantiating `web3` and setting its provider. We will see all of this in more detail very soon, but once again, we have already covered these concepts in previous chapters. The only difference here is that the code is inside of a React environment.

Let's dive into the source code.

Diving into the Truffle and React code

So, the smart contract here is short and simple, and here is the main contract. Inside `contracts/SimpleStorage.sol`, you will find the following content:

```
pragma solidity ^0.4.18;

contract SimpleStorage {
```

```
    uint storedData;

    function set(uint x) public {
      storedData = x;
    }

    function get() public view returns (uint) {
      return storedData;
    }
}
```

As you can see, we have a state variable called `storedData` of the `uint` type. And, we have public `get` and `set` functions.

So, in the UI, to show `The stored value is: 5`, we perform a simple `get`. This is in `src/App.js`:

```
<p>The stored value is: {this.state.storageValue}</p>
```

So, how is all this done? The answer lies in the file that we are looking at. First, note that we import `web3` as usual:

```
import SimpleStorageContract from '../build/contracts/SimpleStorage.json'
import getWeb3 from './utils/getWeb3'
```

Well, not quite. We import from `utils/getWeb3`, which is our abstraction of `web3`. Don't worry, we'll cover this in just a few moments. Let's finish this `App.js` file first.

Notice how we import the JSON of our `SimpleStorage` contract. This is similar to what we did in chapter 1, *Truffle for Decentralized Applications*, where we built a mini decentralized application. Remember, when you compiled your contracts, it created a `build` folder with the JSON representations of each contract.

Now, let's look at the constructor of the `App` class.

```
    constructor(props) {
      super(props)

      this.state = {
        storageValue: 0,
        web3: null
      }
    }
```

We start `web3` off as `null`, with 0 as the initial `storageValue`.

Truffle and Popular JavaScript Technologies

Next, let's take a look at what we do inside the `componentWillMount` function. For more information on this life cycle function, this is a great resource: `https://reactjs.org/docs/react-component.html`.

In short, `componentWillMount` is called once, on the initial render of the page:

```
componentWillMount() {
    // Get network provider and web3 instance.
    // See utils/getWeb3 for more info.

    getWeb3
    .then(results => {
      this.setState({
        web3: results.web3
      })

      // Instantiate contract once web3 provided.
      this.instantiateContract()
    })
    .catch(() => {
      console.log('Error finding web3.')
    })
}
```

`getWeb3` returns a `Promise`. Notice that we have updated the React `state` variable of `web3` with its updated version, by calling `this.setState`. We will dive into `getWeb3` shortly.

After we update the component `state`, we call `this.instantiateContract`. Let's take a look at what happens in there:

```
instantiateContract() {
    /*
     * SMART CONTRACT EXAMPLE
     *
     * Normally these functions would be called in the context of a
     * state management library, but for convenience I've placed them
       here.
     */

    const contract = require('truffle-contract')
    const simpleStorage = contract(SimpleStorageContract)
    simpleStorage.setProvider(this.state.web3.currentProvider)

    // Declaring this for later so we can chain functions on
      SimpleStorage.
```

```
        var simpleStorageInstance

        // Get accounts.
        this.state.web3.eth.getAccounts((error, accounts) => {
          simpleStorage.deployed().then((instance) => {
            simpleStorageInstance = instance

            // Stores a given value, 5 by default.
            return simpleStorageInstance.set(5, {from: accounts[0]})
          }).then((result) => {
            // Get the value from the contract to prove it worked.
            return simpleStorageInstance.get.call(accounts[0])
          }).then((result) => {
            // Update state with the result.
            return this.setState({ storageValue: result.c[0] })
          })
        })
      }
```

As usual, we make use of the JSON of the contract as well as the truffle-contract module to create a usable JavaScript abstraction of our SimpleStorage contract.

```
        const contract = require('truffle-contract')
        const simpleStorage = contract(SimpleStorageContract)
        simpleStorage.setProvider(this.state.web3.currentProvider)
```

Next, we call the getAccounts function of our web3 state variable. On the resolution of the Promise, we call the set function to set a storage value.

```
        return simpleStorageInstance.set(5, {from: accounts[0]})
```

Then, we call the get function to get the value:

```
        return simpleStorageInstance.get.call(accounts[0])
```

Lastly, we call setState again to update our component state and view!

```
        return this.setState({ storageValue: result.c[0] })
```

That's it with web3. Notice there is nothing new that we do with web3 or Truffle here. Once again, the only difference is that we are inside of a React environment, so we make the necessary *React* adjustments.

Great! We've seen how to integrate Truffle with various frontend technologies. But how about the backend? Let's look at how we can call web3 functions and interact with smart contracts from the server side, inside of a Node application.

Truffle and Node

If you skipped the Angular chapter, you need to do the following first:

- Inside your `truffle-practice` folder, create a new folder called `chapter5`

Now, let's get started with Truffle and Node. First, create a new folder called `truffle-node`.

Inside the `truffle-node` folder, we need to initialize a Truffle project.

So, run the following command in your Terminal, while inside the `truffle-node` folder:

`truffle init`

Your `truffle-node` folder structure should now look like this:

```
.
├── contracts
├── migrations
├── test
├── truffle-config.js
└── truffle.js
```

To "run" this Truffle project, we need to have a JavaScript file to run as well as a `package.json` file that states our dependencies. To generate the `package.json` file, simply run `npm init` in your Terminal, while in the `truffle-node` folder.

Now, our folder should have the `package.json` file.

```
.
├── contracts
├── migrations
├── package.json
├── test
├── truffle-config.js
└── truffle.js
```

Next, let's add `web3` as a dependency of this project. To do this, run the following command in your Terminal.

`npm install web3 --save`

You should see `web3` as a dependency added in `package.json` now.

Now, create a file in the root level of your project, and call it `server.js`. This will house all of our web3 and Truffle logic, and it will be the main file that is executed when we "run" our Truffle and Node application.

As usual, let's include an import of `web3`.

```
const Web3 = require("web3");
```

Let's add `http://localhost:8545` as a provider to `web3`.

```
const web3 = new Web3(new
Web3.providers.HttpProvider("http://localhost:8545"));
```

Now, let's write our first piece of `web3` inside of a Node environment. Let's call the `getAccounts` function to get all accounts inside of our local blockchain.

```
web3.eth.getAccounts().then(console.log);
```

Now, it's time to run our Truffle and Node application.

Running our Truffle and Node application

The following set of commands will be referred to as the node run steps. You will reference this later in this section.

The node run steps

1. In a different Terminal window/tab, start a local blockchain by running `ganache-cli`.
2. In another Terminal window, inside the `truffle-node` folder, run our main JavaScript file that we just added a few lines of code to. To do this, run `node server.js` (or use `nodemon`, if you have it installed).

Once you execute the node run steps, you should see accounts listed in your terminal console. In my screen, I see this:

```
[ '0x3D8e65c2d584f2683fA700014bF938ff97317073',
  '0x677773f02690D18a3BFd7ECb89d78D8B1f809050',
  '0xA5651169bfF12D014605C593C9F0C760375b3608',
  '0x69bB6D369171345aB349F66Bc8c5d2c127b537b4',
  '0x2Ef55358d31071f63aFec6e610C6c2c38dF9cD56',
  '0x39EB29716945D3f88650Bf0a96C8cDBb40c9d307',
```

```
    '0x35878EE4dd353b46Bd9Ab65d5e7B48cA625F997f',
    '0x2c8F47646Ac3A208A7e24F95B06f50e0190FFE48',
    '0x8D3417d762641a213418CD43542D2c3bb4F2Eb57',
    'OxAEfdfC779de249f468D60E7A15ae8B641a0Cf55b' ]
```

Great! We've got `web3` working inside of a Node environment; in other words, you have called a `web3` function from the server side!

The fun does not stop here—you can add more of the usual `web3` commands we've already encountered. In fact, let's run the same commands we ran in the `chapter2` folder.

Delete the following line in your `server.js` file:

> web3.eth.getAccounts().then(console.log);

Then, underneath the import statements, paste the following code:

```
web3.eth.getAccounts()
  .then(function (accounts) {
    console.log(JSON.stringify(accounts, null, 2));
    return accounts;
  })
  .then(function (accounts) {
    var firstAccount = accounts[0];
    return web3.eth.getBalance(firstAccount);
  })
  .then(function (accountBalance) {
    console.log('balance in wei: ', accountBalance);
    console.log('balance in ether: ', web3.utils.fromWei(accountBalance,
'ether'));
    return accountBalance;
  })
  .catch(function (error) {
    console.error(error);
  });
```

Essentially, we pasted the same code from our `web3-playground.js` from the `chapter2` folder. For convenience, you can also find the `web3-playground.js` file here: https://github.com/PacktPublishing/Truffle-Quick-Start-Guide/blob/master/chapter2/web3-playground.js.

Execute the Node Run Steps again, and you should see something similar to this in your terminal console:

```
[
  "0x3D8e65c2d584f2683fA700014bF938ff97317073",
  "0x677773f02690D18a3BFd7ECb89d78D8B1f809050",
```

```
    "0xA5651169bfF12D014605C593C9F0C760375b3608",
    "0x69bB6D369171345aB349F66Bc8c5d2c127b537b4",
    "0x2Ef55358d31071f63aFec6e610C6c2c38dF9cD56",
    "0x39EB29716945D3f88650Bf0a96C8cDBb40c9d307",
    "0x35878EE4dd353b46Bd9Ab65d5e7B48cA625F997f",
    "0x2c8F47646Ac3A208A7e24F95B06f50e0190FFE48",
    "0x8D3417d762641a213418CD43542D2c3bb4F2Eb57",
    "0xAEfdfC779de249f468D60E7A15ae8B641a0Cf55b"
]
balance in wei: 100000000000000000000
balance in ether: 100
```

Good job! We've now seen how to interact with `web3` inside of a Node environment.

Now, it's time to interact with a Truffle contract from the server side. To do this, we need a contract first.

Head into the `contracts` folder, and create the same `SimpleStorage` contract we used in the *Truffle and React* section. If you skipped this section, no worries, simply create a file called `SimpleStorage.sol` under `contracts`.

Then, paste the following code:

```
pragma solidity ^0.4.18;

contract SimpleStorage {
  uint storedData;

  function set(uint x) public {
    storedData = x;
  }

  function get() public view returns (uint) {
    return storedData;
  }
}
```

Now let's make sure our `migrations` folder knows about the `SimpleStorage` contract so we can get a proper migration. In `migrations`, create a new file called `2_deploy_contracts.js`.

In that file, paste the following code:

```
var SimpleStorage = artifacts.require("./SimpleStorage.sol");

module.exports = function(deployer) {
  deployer.deploy(SimpleStorage);
```

Truffle and Popular JavaScript Technologies

```
};
```

This should not be new to you. We've done this in previous chapters; we're simply telling Truffle to deploy (migrate) this contract.

Accordingly, it's time to perform a build and migration. While `ganache-cli` is still running, run the following commands in a new Terminal window/tab:

1. `truffle compile` (notice that the `build` folder gets generated)
2. `truffle migrate`

If you have followed the steps correctly so far, you should actually see the following error in your terminal console:

```
Error: No network specified. Cannot determine current network.
```

Well, that's because your `truffle.js` file is empty!

So, in that file, specify a network:

```
module.exports = {
  networks: {
    development: {
      host: 'localhost',
      port: 8545,
      network_id: '*' // Match any network id
    }
  }
}
```

Now, try to migrate our contract again by running `truffle migrate`. You should see a successful migration.

In my terminal console, I see the following:

```
Running migration: 1_initial_migration.js
  Deploying Migrations...
  ... 0x4e2aa3d102f238778b593a280543f9e220004adb179180143f88a2260edb003d
  Migrations: 0x687b71238afd6efd89af5bb50f9a6c7074b568d0
Saving successful migration to network...
  ... 0xa8fae3e34e6ebd03a32a03ccaff493e5cfa1ee29eb5554ab2b62ae46989feddc
Saving artifacts...
Running migration: 2_deploy_contracts.js
  Deploying SimpleStorage...
  ... 0x29332870628b33f64fbfb602cb463cda7185c5c4361191a18a7242a4fc062c3d
  SimpleStorage: 0x36e414404ac1a562a93f52ec834a66216fba3b88
```

```
Saving successful migration to network...
    ... 0x3a88a5cb48f25ba431694ef8255a22416676758b401fdb479f8d0eabe2db021d
Saving artifacts...
```

Great. We've migrated our contract!

Now, let's go back to `server.js` and interact with our freshly deployed contract. But first, let's install `truffle-contract` so we can use it to build the JavaScript abstraction of our contract. In a new terminal window, run the following command:

`npm install truffle-contract`

Then, under the `web3` import, paste the following code:

```
const contract = require('truffle-contract');
```

Then, let's import the JSON of our contract:

```
const SimpleStorageContract =
require('./build/contracts/SimpleStorage.json');
```

Using `truffle-contract` and the JSON of our contract, we can create the JavaScript representation of our contract:

```
const simpleStorage = contract(SimpleStorageContract);
simpleStorage.setProvider(web3.currentProvider);
```

Now, let's declare some variables to store the deployed instance of our contract as well as the first account from our list of accounts. You'll see very soon why this is necessary. After all of the import statements, and before the `web3` commands, add the following code

```
var simpleStorageInstance, firstAccount;
```

Then, let's call the `get` and `set` public functions of the contract instance. You can add the following chain of `then` instances after your final `web3 then` and before the `catch`.

```
.then(function () {
  return simpleStorage.deployed();
})
.then(function (instance) {
  simpleStorageInstance = instance;
  return simpleStorageInstance.set(5, {from: firstAccount});
})
.then(function (result) {
  return simpleStorageInstance.get.call({
    from:firstAccount
  });
```

```
    })
    .then(function (result) {
      console.log(+result)
      return result;
    })
```

If that was confusing, your full chain of `then` instances should look like this:

```
web3.eth.getAccounts()
  .then(function (accounts) {
    accounts = accounts;
    console.log(JSON.stringify(accounts, null, 2));
    return accounts;
  })
  .then(function (accounts) {
    firstAccount = accounts[0];
    return web3.eth.getBalance(firstAccount);
  })
  .then(function (accountBalance) {
    console.log('balance in wei: ', accountBalance);
    console.log('balance in ether: ',
    web3.utils.fromWei(accountBalance, 'ether'));
    return accountBalance;
  })
  .then(function () {
    return simpleStorage.deployed();
  })
  .then(function (instance) {
    simpleStorageInstance = instance;
    return simpleStorageInstance.set(5, {from: firstAccount});
  })
  .then(function (result) {
    return simpleStorageInstance.get.call({
      from:firstAccount
    });
  })
  .then(function (result) {
    console.log(+result)
    return result;
  })
  .catch(function (error) {
    console.error(error);
  });
```

Now, perform the Node Run Steps. Don't break your computer, because you may still see an error! Specifically, you may see this:

`TypeError: Cannot read property 'apply' of undefined`

At the time of writing this book, there is an open GitHub issue related to this being a bug with web3 version 1 and above. The `web3` version in my project for this section is `^1.0.0-beta.33`. You can read more about this issue here: `https://github.com/trufflesuite/truffle-contract/issues/57`.

Like most problems, this problem has a workaround. After your import statements, paste the following code:

```
if (typeof simpleStorage.currentProvider.sendAsync !== "function") {
  simpleStorage.currentProvider.sendAsync = function() {
    return simpleStorage.currentProvider.send.apply(
      simpleStorage.currentProvider, arguments
    );
  };
}
```

Your entire `server.js` file should now look like this:

```
const Web3 = require('web3');
const contract = require('truffle-contract');
const web3 = new Web3(new
Web3.providers.HttpProvider('http://localhost:8545'));
const SimpleStorageContract =
require('./build/contracts/SimpleStorage.json');
const simpleStorage = contract(SimpleStorageContract)
simpleStorage.setProvider(web3.currentProvider)
if (typeof simpleStorage.currentProvider.sendAsync !== "function") {
  simpleStorage.currentProvider.sendAsync = function() {
    return simpleStorage.currentProvider.send.apply(
      simpleStorage.currentProvider, arguments
    );
  };
}

var simpleStorageInstance, firstAccount;

web3.eth.getAccounts()
  .then(function (accounts) {
    accounts = accounts;
    console.log(JSON.stringify(accounts, null, 2));
    return accounts;
  })
```

```
  .then(function (accounts) {
    firstAccount = accounts[0];
    return web3.eth.getBalance(firstAccount);
  })
  .then(function (accountBalance) {
    console.log('balance in wei: ', accountBalance);
    console.log('balance in ether: ', web3.utils.fromWei(accountBalance,
'ether'));
    return accountBalance;
  })
  .then(function () {
    return simpleStorage.deployed();
  })
  .then(function (instance) {
    simpleStorageInstance = instance;
    return simpleStorageInstance.set(5, {from: firstAccount});
  })
  .then(function (result) {
    return simpleStorageInstance.get.call({
      from:firstAccount
    });
  })
  .then(function (result) {
    console.log(+result)
    return result;
  })
  .catch(function (error) {
    console.error(error);
  });
```

You can also find the full `server.js` file here: https://github.com/PacktPublishing/Truffle-Quick-Start-Guide/blob/master/chapter5/truffle-node/server.js.

Now, if you perform the *node run steps* section again, you should see a similar output to this in your terminal output:

```
[
  "0x3D8e65c2d584f2683fA700014bF938ff97317073",
  "0x677773f02690D18a3BFd7ECb89d78D8B1f809050",
  "0xA5651169bfF12D014605C593C9F0C760375b3608",
  "0x69bB6D369171345aB349F66Bc8c5d2c127b537b4",
  "0x2Ef55358d31071f63aFec6e610C6c2c38dF9cD56",
  "0x39EB29716945D3f88650Bf0a96C8cDBb40c9d307",
  "0x35878EE4dd353b46Bd9Ab65d5e7B48cA625F997f",
  "0x2c8F47646Ac3A208A7e24F95B06f50e0190FFE48",
  "0x8D3417d762641a213418CD43542D2c3bb4F2Eb57",
  "0xAEfdfC779de249f468D60E7A15ae8B641a0Cf55b"
```

```
]
balance in wei: 99955263899999771864
balance in ether: 99.955263899999771864
5
```

Great job! We've now interacted with Truffle and `web3` from the server side, inside of a Node environment!

Summary

This was quite the chapter! We got our hands dirty with Angular, React, and Node. As you have seen, we did nothing new with `web3` or Truffle. We simply interacted with them the way we have done before, with the only difference being that we were inside of Angular, React, and Node environments.

Being able to integrate Truffle and `web3` with modern JavaScript frameworks is key to becoming a well-versed and seasoned smart contract developer. You're well on your way!

See you in the next chapter, where you will learn an essential skill that is useful not only when writing smart contracts, but production-level software in general—unit tests.

6
Testing Your Dapp

This chapter will introduce you to the importance of thoroughly testing your smart contracts, as well as various techniques and approaches for successfully testing a Truffle application. Specifically, this chapter will cover how to write comprehensive unit tests in Solidity and JavaScript, as well as the correct method for testing modifiers and reverts. Moreover, this chapter will illustrate how to test for events being thrown in your Solidity contract too. You will also learn about fundamental concepts, such as transaction objects and parameters, when working with `truffle-contract` and `web3`.

In particular, you will learn how to do the following:

- Write comprehensive unit tests in Solidity
- Write comprehensive unit tests in JavaScript
- Test Solidity events

Unit tests are a great way to test whether your contract works as expected, rather than learning the hard way in production.

Firstly, how do we approach writing unit tests in general?

When writing a unit test, you have to isolate the piece of logic you want to test. That's why it's called a *unit* test. This is best illustrated with an example, and we will see several in this chapter. As you progress through this chapter, you will learn that JavaScript tests are generally more flexible and powerful than Solidity tests.

As you may have guessed by now, there are two options when you are writing unit tests for a smart contract. You can write tests either in Solidity or JavaScript—in fact, you can use both! Let's get started with writing unit tests in Solidity.

Technical requirements

You will be required to have basic knowledge of JavaScript and web development as well as Ethereum/blockchain. Finally, to use the Git repository of this book, the user needs to install Git.

The code files for this chapter can be found on GitHub:
`https://github.com/PacktPublishing/Truffle-Quick-Start-Guide/tree/master/Chapter06`

Check out the following video to see the code in action:
`http://bit.ly/2KaSGO7`

Writing unit tests with Solidity

Before we start the exercises in this chapter, let's do the usual housekeeping:

- Inside your `truffle-practice` folder, create a new folder called `chapter6`

Great! That's it. Let's get started with this chapter. Now, we've already built a few mini applications, so which one should we write tests for? Let's write tests for the mini-application we wrote in Chapter 1, *Truffle for Decentralized Applications*. Why? There are two reasons:

- The Chapter 1, *Truffle for Decentralized Applications*, project contains fundamental Solidity elements that we should write tests for.
- The Chapter 1, *Truffle for Decentralized Applications*, project does not rely on a particular JavaScript framework. Since it's in VanillaJS, you can just focus on writing unit tests without worrying about framework-specific caveats.

Since we are writing tests for the Chapter 1, *Truffle for Decentralized Applications*, application, let's copy the contents of our `chapter1` folder into our `chapter6` folder. Then, to ensure it runs, perform the following steps:

1. `cd chapter6`
2. `rm -rf build`
3. `truffle develop`

4. Inside the Truffle development console, run the following:
    1. `compile` (this compiles our contracts)
    2. `migrate` (this migrates our contract to the network specified in `truffle.js`)
5. Navigate to `http://localhost:8081/#/`

Ensure the applications run as usual and that there are no errors. Everything should work smoothly, as we are simply taking working code from Chapter 1, *Truffle for Decentralized Applications*, and running it.

Let's take a look at the `reward` function in the `TaskMaster` contract. Under contracts, inside the `TaskMaster.sol` file, observe the following function:

```
function reward(address doer, uint rewardAmount)
    public
    isOwner()
    hasSufficientFunds(rewardAmount)
    returns(bool sufficientFunds)
{
    balances[msg.sender] -= rewardAmount;
    balances[doer] += rewardAmount;
    return sufficientFunds;
}
```

It's a simple function that involves some accounting and a superficial transfer of `wei` from one account to another. However, there is a lot we can test for. Firstly, we can test whether the accounting is being done correctly. Secondly, we can test whether the modifiers `isOwner` and `hasSufficientFunds` are correctly reverting the function. But before we get into this, let's take an easier example.

Let's test the most basic function—the constructor. After all, if the constructor does not run as expected, your contract is destined for failure.

Let's take a look at our constructor:

```
function TaskMaster() public {
    balances[msg.sender] = 10000;
    owner = msg.sender;
}
```

We have assigned a balance of `10000 wei` to the sender of the function. So, let's see whether this action takes place.

Testing the TaskMaster

Under the `test` folder, you should already see two test files, one in JavaScript and one in Solidity. These were the files that came out of the box when we initialized our Truffle project. Since we have a `TaskMaster` contract and not a `MetaCoin` contract, feel free to delete those two test files. Let's start from scratch.

Your `test` folder should now be empty.

Now, inside the `test` folder, create a new file called `TestTaskMaster.sol`.

It is good practice to prefix your Solidity test files with *Test* before the name of the contract you are testing. So, if you are testing a contract called `TaskMaster`, it is good practice to name your test contract `TestTaskMaster`.

Start by adding a few necessary Truffle imports, including a file that allows us to make assertions:

```
pragma solidity ^0.4.17;

import "truffle/Assert.sol";
import "truffle/DeployedAddresses.sol";
import "../contracts/TaskMaster.sol";
```

As mentioned, the first imported file allows us to make assertions. If this is confusing to you, worry not—it will make a lot more sense when we write our first test.

The second imported file, `truffle/DeployedAddresses.sol`, allows us to get and use the deployed addresses of contracts from our `migrations` folder. This is not always necessary, as you will see later on in this section. But, when trying to test specific deployed contracts, it will come in handy.

The third imported file is simply our contract. Of course, we need this to write tests as we will be calling public functions from `TaskMaster`.

Next, let's create our test contract and a function that will hold the logic of our test for the initial balance:

```
contract TestTaskMaster {
  function testInitialBalance() {
  }
}
```

The first thing we need is an instance of `TaskMaster`. So, let's use `DeployedAddresses` to get the deployed address of our `TaskMaster` contract. And using that address, we can *revive* an instance of `TaskMaster`, as follows:

```
TaskMaster taskMaster = TaskMaster(DeployedAddresses.TaskMaster());
```

Place the preceding line inside the `testInitialBalance` function.

Next, let's define and initialize the variable that will hold the value that we expect to have as our initial balance. Underneath the contract instantiation, paste the following line:

```
uint expectedBalance = 10000;
```

A unit test is only a unit test with an expected and actual comparison. So, let's define and initialize a variable that will hold our actual balance value. Underneath the expected balance, add the following line of code:

```
uint actualBalance = taskMaster.getBalance(taskMaster.owner());
```

A few things are going on here. First, we call the `getBalance` public function of the `TaskMaster` contract to get the owner's balance. How can we call this now?

> Since `owner` is a `public` variable of the `TaskMaster` contract, we can access it via a built-in `owner` function.
>
> For more information on `getter` and `setter` methods for `public` variables in Solidity, the following resource is useful: http://solidity.readthedocs.io/en/develop/contracts.html?#visibility-and-getters.

If you recall, we already initialized our contract on the first line inside `testInitialBalance`! So, if things go as planned, the balance should already be set.

Let's add our final line now, to test whether our actual balance is equal to our expected balance:

```
Assert.equal(actualBalance, expectedBalance, "Owner should have 10000 wei");
```

Testing Your Dapp

As you can see, we use `Assert` to check whether our actual balance is equal to our expected balance. And, in case they are not equal, we specify an error message to be displayed in the third argument.

Your entire `testInitialBalance` function should look like this:

```
contract TestTaskMaster {
  function testInitialBalance() {
    TaskMaster taskMaster = TaskMaster(DeployedAddresses.TaskMaster());
    uint expectedBalance = 10000;
    uint actualBalance = taskMaster.getBalance(taskMaster.owner());
    Assert.equal(actualBalance, expectedBalance, "Owner should have
    10000 wei");
}
```

When writing unit tests, it is great practice to make clear and explicitly state the *expected* value and the *actual* value.

Looking at the previous code, this may seem redundant, but as tests get more complex, it is very helpful to outline clearly what the expected value and actual value are.

Now, let's run our test to see whether we are in the green.

Ensure you are in the Truffle development console. Once you are in, simply run `test`. You should see the following output in your Terminal console:

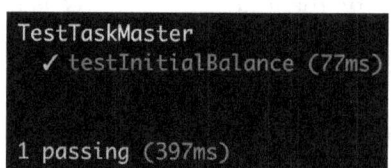

Before we write more tests, let's just see what a failing test looks like. In your `testInitialBalance` function, change `expectedBalance` to `10001`.

Then, run your test file again. In your Terminal console, you should see the following output:

```
TestTaskMaster
  1) testInitialBalance

  Events emitted during test:
  ---------------------------

  TestEvent(result: <indexed>, message: Owner should have 10000 wei (Tested: 10000, Against: 10001))

  ---------------------------

0 passing (607ms)
1 failing

1) TestTaskMaster testInitialBalance:
   Error: Owner should have 10000 wei (Tested: 10000, Against: 10001)
     at /Users/nikhilwins/.nvm/versions/node/v6.12.0/lib/node_modules/truffle/build/cli.bundled.js:319138:17
     at Array.forEach (native)
     at processResult (/Users/nikhilwins/.nvm/versions/node/v6.12.0/lib/node_modules/truffle/build/cli.bundled
.js:319136:19)
     at process._tickDomainCallback (internal/process/next_tick.js:135:7)
```

As you can see, it says `0 passing` and `1 failing`. Moreover, we see our error message, `Owner should have 10000 wei`, being displayed.

> When writing unit tests, it is good practice to see them fail before you make them succeed. The reason for this is that you will occasionally run into cases where you have *false positive* tests. In other words, your tests may pass *unintentionally* because of an error you made.
>
> Therefore, seeing your test fail before you make it pass is a great way to ensure that your passing tests are *true positive*.

Let's test our `reward` function:

```
function reward(address doer, uint rewardAmount)
    public
    isOwner()
    hasSufficientFunds(rewardAmount)
    returns(bool sufficientFunds)
{
    balances[msg.sender] -= rewardAmount;
    balances[doer] += rewardAmount;
    return sufficientFunds;
}
```

Testing Your Dapp

A few things are happening here. Firstly, we decrement the sender's balance by the reward amount. Secondly, we increment the receiver's amount by the reward amount. Moreover, this function is modified by `isOwner` and `hasSufficientFunds`.

As a reminder, `isOwner` ensures that the sender (`msg.sender`) of the contract is the owner of the contract. `hasSufficientFunds` ensures that the reward amount being sent is less than or equal to the sender's balance.

So, let's write a test to ensure that all of this happens. First, inside the `TestTaskMaster` contract, create a function called `testReward`. Inside this function, initialize the contract using `DeployedAddresses` like we did before:

```
function testReward() {
    TaskMaster taskMaster = new TaskMaster();
}
```

Notice how we don't use `DeployedAddresses` here. We want to create a brand new instance of `TaskMaster` because we want to be able to test for owner and recipient logic. This is not actually necessary, but when testing for updates of `state` variables, it's good practice to start with a fresh contract. This is also good practice when writing unit tests in general.

Next, we need an address that we want to send a reward to. Any valid Ethereum address will do. I use the address `0xE0f5206BBD039e7b0592d8918820024e2a7437b9`. Feel free to use it too. Underneath the contract instantiation, paste the following line:

```
address recipientAddress = 0xE0f5206BBD039e7b0592d8918820024e2a7437b9;
```

As a next step, we have to set the reward amount. Let's set an amount less than our owner's balance of `10000`. I set `50` as the reward amount. Beneath the recipient address initialization, paste the following line:

```
uint rewardAmount = 50;
```

Now that we have the recipient address and reward amount, let's actually call the `reward` function. Below the reward amount declaration, paste the following line:

```
taskMaster.reward(recipientAddress, rewardAmount);
```

The meat of our unit test is now done!

Now, as usual, we should set the expected final balance amount for the recipient as well as the owner. We expect the recipient to have a balance of 50 once the transaction is complete. As for the owner, we expect them to have 10000 - 50, which is 9950. So, below the reward invocation, add the following line:

```
uint expectedRecipientBalance = 50;
```

Now, we need to define and initialize a variable that will hold the actual final value of the recipient's balance. To get the recipient's balance, let's call the getBalance function. Underneath the last line you pasted, add the following line:

```
uint actualRecipientBalance = taskMaster.getBalance(recipientAddress);
```

What's next? You guessed it, our assertion! Let's test that the recipient's expected balance is equal to the recipient's actual balance:

```
Assert.equal(actualRecipientBalance, expectedRecipientBalance, "Recipient should have 50 wei");
```

Let's run our tests. You should see both tests pass:

```
TestTaskMaster
  ✓ testInitialBalance (55ms)
  ✓ testReward (93ms)

2 passing (427ms)
```

For good measure, change the `expectedRecipientBalance` to, say, 49. Run your tests again and hopefully they will fail!

Great! Now, I'll leave it as an exercise for you to test whether the owner's balance is updated correctly!

Take your time.

Are you done? Good job! Your final `testReward` function should look like this:

```
function testReward() {
    TaskMaster taskMaster = new TaskMaster();

    address recipientAddress = 0xE0f5206BBD039e7b0592d8918820024e2a7437b9;
    uint rewardAmount = 50;
    taskMaster.reward(recipientAddress, rewardAmount);
```

[125]

Testing Your Dapp

```
        uint expectedRecipientBalance = 50;
        uint actualRecipientBalance =
        taskMaster.getBalance(recipientAddress);
        Assert.equal(actualRecipientBalance, expectedRecipientBalance,
        "Recipient should have 50 wei");

        uint expectedOwnerBalance = 9950;
        uint actualOwnerBalance =
         taskMaster.getBalance(taskMaster.owner());
        Assert.equal(actualOwnerBalance, expectedOwnerBalance, "Owner
        should have 9950 wei");
    }
```

Great job! Looks like we are now starting to get the hang of writing unit tests.

How about testing whether our modifiers, `isOwner` and `hasSuffucientFunds`, work as expected? Specifically, we have to test for whether the modifiers cause the transaction to revert when either of them fail.

While this is possible in Solidity tests, it is not standardized. There are a few third-party implementations of tests for `revert`, `assert` or `require` statements. However, they are just that—third-party. Therefore, they may break or not work as Solidity or the EVM changes/updates. Regardless, if you would like to try writing these for yourself, you can check out the following article, which provides a solid foundation for writing your own tests for transaction reversions and more: http://truffleframework.com/tutorials/testing-for-throws-in-solidity-tests.

That being said, we will see how to test modifiers and reversions in the next section of this chapter when we write JavaScript tests for our contract! It turns out that testing for reversions in JavaScript is a smoother process; we will see how this is done in the next section.

We've covered a lot in this section. You have learned how to unit test your smart contract functions. Of course, this contract is still relatively simple compared to the ones you will encounter. To learn more about Solidity unit tests, you can check out http://truffleframework.com/tutorials/solidity-unit-tests.

You can find all of the code we did for this chapter here: https://github.com/PacktPublishing/Truffle-Quick-Start-Guide/tree/master/chapter6.

Now, let's write unit tests in JavaScript.

Writing unit tests with JavaScript

Inside the contracts folder, create a `.js` file that will house our tests; call it `test-task-master.js`.

Again, stick to the same practice of prepending our contract name with the word `test` so that it's clear that it's a `test` file. I prefer JavaScript file names to be snake case, but if you prefer camelCase file names, that is fine too.

Inside the `test-task-master.js` file, let's import our contract so we can make use of it in our tests:

```
const TaskMaster = artifacts.require("../contracts/TaskMaster.sol");
```

`artifacts` is automatically injected by Truffle inside our test environment, and it allows us to instantiate our contract easily for the purpose of testing.

Next, let's define a function where we will place all of the unit tests of our contract. Underneath the `artifacts.require` statement, add the following block of code:

```
contract('TaskMaster', accounts => {
  console.log(accounts);
});
```

`contract` is a function that will house all of the unit tests for a particular contract. Like `artifacts`, it is injected by Truffle tests.

Let's look at the arguments of the `contract` function:

- The first argument is a string where you specify the name of the contract. Here, we passed in `TaskMaster` because that is the name of the contract we are testing.
- The second argument is a callback function that will house all of our tests, local variables, and pre- and post-test configurations. As you can see, the `accounts` array gets passed in by Truffle as an argument to the callback function. This `accounts` array will hold all of the accounts associated with the blockchain we are connected to, as we have seen before.

Run the Truffle tests. If you skipped the previous *Writing unit tests with Solidity* section, you can *run* the Truffle tests doing the following:

1. `cd chapter6`
2. `truffle develop`
3. Inside the Truffle development console, run `test`

Testing Your Dapp

In your console, you should see the accounts being printed out:

```
[ '0x627306090abab3a6e1400e9345bc60c78a8bef57',
  '0xf17f52151ebef6c7334fad080c5704d77216b732',
  '0xc5fdf4076b8f3a5357c5e395ab970b5b54098fef',
  '0x821aea9a577a9b44299b9c15c88cf3087f3b5544',
  '0x0d1d4e623d10f9fba5db95830f7d3839406c6af2',
  '0x2932b7a2355d6fecc4b5c0b6bd44cc31df247a2e',
  '0x2191ef87e392377ec08e7c08eb105ef5448eced5',
  '0x0f4f2ac550a1b4e2280d04c21cea7ebd822934b5',
  '0x6330a553fc93768f612722bb8c2ec78ac90b3bbc',
  '0x5aeda56215b167893e80b4fe645ba6d5bab767de' ]
```

This is a good start. Now that we've ensured that Truffle recognizes our JavaScript test file and has connected to a local blockchain, we can start writing tests.

You can remove the `console.log` statement. Inside the contract's second argument (the function) paste the following code:

```
let owner, recipient;

before("should set owner", () => {
    assert.isAtLeast(accounts.length, 2, 'There should be at least 2 accounts');
    owner = accounts[0];
    recipient = accounts[1];
});
```

What's going on here?:

- First, we declare variables to hold the owner and recipient of the contract.
- Then, we open a `before` block. `before`, as its name suggests, will be executed **before** all tests get executed. So, a `before` block is perfect for doing some global preparation that all of our tests will depend on. Like `contract`, `before` is a function that is injected by Truffle to be used inside our test environment.

The first thing we do is to make use of the `assert` function. Like `before` and `contract`, `assert` is injected by Truffle. We *assert* that there are at least two accounts present in our local blockchain. Why? We need at least two accounts: one owner and one recipient.

Chapter 6

We call the `isAtLeast` function of `assert` to assert that `accounts.length` is of at least length 2.

If it is not, we will see `"There should be at least 2 accounts"` displayed in our terminal console.

Your entire file should now look like this:

```
const TaskMaster = artifacts.require("../contracts/TaskMaster.sol");

contract('TaskMaster', accounts => {

  let owner, recipient;

  before("should set owner", () => {
      assert.isAtLeast(accounts.length, 2, 'There should be at least 2
        accounts');
      owner = accounts[0];
      recipient = accounts[1];
  });

});
```

We assign the first account to `owner` and the second to `recipient`.

You can run this, but you won't see anything in your terminal console because we don't even have actual tests written for the `before` statement to execute!

Let's write our first test. As usual, let's first test that the constructor of `TaskMaster` works as expected, and that the contract state gets properly initialized.

Underneath the `before` statement, paste the following code:

```
it("should set owner balance", function() {
  const expectedOwnerBalance = 10000;
  let instance;

  return TaskMaster.deployed()
    .then(_instance => {
        instance = _instance;
        return instance.getBalance(owner, { from: owner });
    })
});
```

Testing Your Dapp

> **TIP**: If you would like to use ES7's (ECMAScript 2016) `async/await` pattern instead of chaining `then` statements, go ahead!

The fundamentals of writing JavaScript tests are still the same.

`it` is a function injected by Truffle. Let's take a look at its arguments:

- The first argument is a string, and it is meant to represent what the test is trying to enforce. Read it like a sentence—`should set owner balance`.
- The second argument is a callback function that will house our actual test.

Inside the callback function, you can see that we have declared and initialized a variable to hold the expected value of the owner's balance upon deployment of the contract.

Underneath the variable declarations, we call `TaskMaster.deployed()`. This returns a `Promise` that resolves to a usable instance of this contract.

Also, it is important to note that when `TaskMaster.deployed()` gets called, the constructor of `TaskMaster` gets called with `msg.sender` as the first account in the `accounts` array.

Once we set the instance variable, we make a call to get the balance of the contract owner:

```
.then(_instance => {
    instance = _instance;
    return instance.getBalance.call(owner, { from: owner });
})
```

`getBalance` takes one argument, the account/address that we want to get the balance for. However, we pass in a second argument here, as you can see:

```
{ from: owner }
```

These objects hold the **transaction parameters**. They specify some additional details about the transaction, including the sender of the message and the gas to be used. We will see more of this later in this section. It is also important to note that passing in this transaction parameter is *optional*. For more information about the transaction object, this resource is helpful: `https://github.com/ethereum/wiki/wiki/JavaScript-API#web3ethsendtransaction`.

`getBalance` also returns a `Promise`, so let's add another `then` to get the `Promise` resolution:

```
.then(actualOwnerBalance => {
    assert.equal(actualOwnerBalance, expectedOwnerBalance, `Owner should have ${expectedOwnerBalance}`);
    return;
});
```

Here, we assert that the actual owner's balance is equal to what we expected the owner's balance to be.

Run your test!

You should see it pass; this is indicated by the green checkmark:

✓ should set owner balance

In case you skipped the *Writing unit tests in Solidity* section, when writing unit tests, it is good practice to see them fail before you make them succeed.

The reason for this is that you will occasionally run into cases where you have false positive tests. In other words, your tests may pass unintentionally because of an error you made.

So, always ensure you see your tests fail with intentionally failing cases before you see or make them pass.

Great! Remember, you can access the full `test-task-master.js` file here: https://github.com/PacktPublishing/Truffle-Quick-Start-Guide/blob/master/chapter6/test/test-task-master.js.

Now let's test the `reward` function. Just to recall, here's what that function looks like:

```
function reward(address doer, uint rewardAmount)
    public
    isOwner()
    hasSufficientFunds(rewardAmount)
    returns(bool sufficientFunds)
{
    balances[msg.sender] -= rewardAmount;
```

Testing Your Dapp

```
        balances[doer] += rewardAmount;
        return sufficientFunds;
}
```

We want to test whether it correctly increments the owner and recipient accounts. Also, we should test whether the `isOwner` and `hasSufficientFunds` work as expected.

Underneath the first `it` block, create another one, as follows:

```
it("should be able to reward recipient", function() {

});
```

As you may have guessed, this ensures that the `reward` function works as expected. Inside the callback function of this `it` block, let's declare and assign variables that will hold the original owner balance, original recipient balance, and the reward amount.

```
const REWARD_WEI = 50;
let originalOwnerBalance;
let originalRecipientBalance;
let instance;
```

Underneath these variable declarations, let's deploy our contract as usual.

Then, we can get the original balances of the owner and the recipient. We can use these values to compare to the final values to see if their respective balances incremented and decremented by the exact reward amount.

In the `Promise` resolution, get the original balances of the owner and the recipient.

```
        return TaskMaster.deployed()
          .then(_instance => {
            instance = _instance;
            return instance.getBalance.call(owner, { from: owner } );
        })
          .then(_originalOwnerBalance => {
            originalOwnerBalance = _originalOwnerBalance;
            return instance.getBalance.call(recipient, { from: owner } );
        })
```

Then, call the `reward` function:

```
.then(_originalRecipientBalance => {
  originalRecipientBalance = _originalRecipientBalance;
  return instance.reward(recipient, REWARD_WEI, {
    from: owner
```

```
    });
})
```

The `reward` function takes two arguments, the recipient and the reward amount.

Of course, we pass in a third argument, which is a JavaScript object holding transaction parameters. We are setting `msg.sender` as the owner. This is good, as the `isOwner()` modifier requires that the sender of the transaction is the owner of the contract.

Once the `Promise` resolves, the transaction is complete. So, let's see if the owner's and recipient's balances changed by the reward amount!

```
.then(rewardTxObj => {
    return instance.getBalance.call(owner, { from: owner } );
})
.then(actualOwnerBalance => {
    assert.equal(actualOwnerBalance.toNumber(), +originalOwnerBalance - REWARD_WEI, `Owner should have ${REWARD_WEI} less`);
    return instance.getBalance.call(recipient, { from: owner } );
})
.then(actualRecipientBalance => {
    assert.equal(actualRecipientBalance.toNumber(), +originalRecipientBalance + REWARD_WEI, `Recipient should have ${REWARD_WEI} more`);
    return;
});
```

You may be wondering what `rewardTxObj` is. Once the Promise of reward resolves a transaction, the return value of that transaction is a transaction object. Here's what the transaction object of the `reward` function looks like:

```
{ tx: '0x1d763100bef073a7cccfa2eba36ab510d234ad368d5977f9010b3c9eb30c0fbf',
  receipt:
   { transactionHash: '0x1d763100bef073a7cccfa2eba36ab510d234ad368d5977f9010b3c9eb30c0fbf',
     transactionIndex: 0,
     blockHash: '0x390aa9e46b6f70017aba58dd5b4c92d2d501ffe56cb0fcb374c58345d9a87e34',
     blockNumber: 30,
     gasUsed: 49396,
     cumulativeGasUsed: 49396,
     contractAddress: null,
     logs: [],
     status: 1 },
  logs: [] }
```

Testing Your Dapp

You will notice that for a `view` function like `getBalance`, the transaction object is not returned. This is because `getBalance` does not execute a transaction! Remember, a `view` function does not modify the state of the contract and in turn does not trigger a transaction. Only transactions return transaction objects once their `Promise` resolves.

As for the rest of the code inside this `it` block, it should all be familiar to you. We are getting the balances of the owner and recipient by calling `getBalance`.

Run the tests. You should see them pass:

```
✓ should set owner balance
✓ should be able to reward recipient (57ms)
```

Now, let's test whether `isOwner` works. To recall, this modifier ensures that *only* the owner can call the `reward` function.

Here it is defined:

```
modifier isOwner() {
    require(msg.sender == owner);
    _;
}
```

And here, the modifier is being used, modifying the `reward` function:

```
function reward(address doer, uint rewardAmount)
    public
    isOwner()
    hasSufficientFunds(rewardAmount)
    returns(bool sufficientFunds)
{
    balances[msg.sender] -= rewardAmount;
    balances[doer] += rewardAmount;
    return sufficientFunds;
}
```

So, we must ensure that our transaction reverts if someone other than `owner` tries to test this. To do this, we need a utility function.

At the time of writing this book, a built-in utility function from `truffle-contract` or `web3` that tests for exceptions and reverts thrown by the EVM does not exist.

So, we must look to the Google search bar. I found a good utility function here: https://gist.github.com/xavierlepretre/d5583222fde52ddfbc58b7cfa0d2d0a9.

To prepare, create a folder called `util` in the root level of your project; this folder should be in the same level as for `test`. Inside the `util` folder, create a file called `expected-exception-promise.js`. As the name suggests, this file contains and exports a function to call when we are expecting an exception to be thrown by the EVM.

Inside the file, paste the following code:

```
module.exports = function expectedExceptionPromise(action, gasToUse) {
    return new Promise(function (resolve, reject) {
        try {
            resolve(action());
        } catch(e) {
            reject(e);
        }
    })
    .then(function (txObj) {
        return typeof txn === "string"
            ? web3.eth.getTransactionReceiptMined(txObj) // regular
              tx hash
            : typeof txObj.receipt !== "undefined"
                ? txObj.receipt // truffle-contract function call
                : typeof txObj.transactionHash === "string"
                    ? web3.eth.getTransactionReceiptMined(
                        txObj.transactionHash) //
                        deployment : txObj; // Unknown last case
    })
    .then(function (receipt) {
        // We are in Geth or the tx wrongly passed
        assert.equal(receipt.gasUsed, gasToUse, "should have used
        all the gas");
    })
    .catch(function (e) {
        if ((e + "").indexOf("invalid JUMP") > -1 ||
            (e + "").indexOf("out of gas") > -1 ||
            (e + "").indexOf("revert") > -1 ||
            (e + "").indexOf("invalid opcode") > -1) {
            // We are in TestRPC
        } else if ((e + "").indexOf("please check your gas
          amount")> -1) {
            // We are in Geth for a deployment
        } else {
            throw e;
        }
    });
};
```

Testing Your Dapp

There is no need to go too deep into this code. We just need to know that it looks for signs like `revert` or `invalid opcode` to determine whether an exception was indeed thrown by the EVM.

The first argument of the function is a callback function. You will see how this is used in just a moment.

Notice the second argument of `exceptedExceptionPromise`. We specify a gas amount to be used up by the transaction. If the transaction indeed reverts, all gas is used up. Once again, you will see how this is used shortly.

The function is appended with the word `Promise` because we return all of this logic inside a `Promise`. This way, when we use the function, we simply do `then` to get the resolved result.

Let's make use of `exceptedExceptionPromise`. At the top of the `test-task-master.js` file, below the first `require` statement, add the following line to import `expectedExceptionPromise`:

```
const expectedExceptionPromise = require('../util/expected-exception-
promise.js');
```

Inside the `contract` block, let's write a new unit test. Let's first test the `isOwner` modifier.

In other words, let's see whether the EVM causes a revert when someone other than the owner tries to call the `reward` function.

Remember, the `reward` function is modified by `isOwner`, so only the owner of the contract should be able to call it. Paste the following test inside `contract`:

```
it('should only allow owner to reward', function() {
  const REWARD_WEI = 50;
  let instance;

  return TaskMaster.deployed()
    .then(_instance => {
      instance = _instance;
      return expectedExceptionPromise(
        () => instance.reward(recipient, REWARD_WEI, { from: recipient,
          gas: 3000000 }),
        3000000
      );
```

```
    })
});
```

Everything here should be familiar to you except the use of `expectedExceptionPromise`. As you can see, inside the `callback` function of `expectedExceptionPromise`, we pass in a call to `reward`.

Notice the transaction parameters here:

```
{ from: recipient, gas: 3000000 }
```

First of all, we are making the recipient call the `reward` function. This should not be allowed according to the `isOwner` modifier.

Second, we are passing a gas limit of `3000000`. When the EVM throws a revert, all gas is lost by the sender of the transaction.

This is why in the second argument of `exceptedExceptionPromise`, we pass in `3000000`. We expect all gas to be used up.

Run the test. You should see it pass, as follows:

> ✓ should only allow owner to reward

To ensure this test is actually doing what we want it to do, let's change the `from` transaction parameter from `recipient` to `owner`. The test should now fail. Why? Because we don't expect the EVM to revert when `owner` calls `reward`!

Take a few minutes to wrap your head around this.

Next, let's test the modifier `hasSufficientFunds`.

Under the previous test, write a new test:

```
it('should not be able to reward recipient with reward that exceeds owner
balance', function() {
  const REWARD_WEI = 10001;
  let instance;

  return TaskMaster.deployed()
    .then(_instance => {
      instance = _instance;
      return expectedExceptionPromise(
```

Testing Your Dapp

```
            () => instance.reward(recipient, REWARD_WEI, { from: owner,
              gas: 3000000 }),
            3000000
        );
    })
});
```

Conceptually, the same thing is happening here. We wrap the `reward` function inside our `expectedExceptionPromise` function.

Notice the reward amount we plan to send:

```
const REWARD_WEI = 10001;
```

This is obviously more than the owner's balance of `10000`. Therefore, the test should pass as we are *expecting* the EVM to throw a revert.

Run the test. Again, you should see it pass as follows:

> ✓ should not be able to reward recipient with reward that exceeds owner balance

That's it! We have now tested both modifiers of `TaskMaster`.

And of course, we've tested both public functions of the contract too.

> When testing for a failure, you must ensure that all other parts of the function, other than the case you are testing for, work. For example, when we tested `isOwner`, we ensured that there were indeed sufficient funds in the transaction. This way, we only need test for `isOwner`. Conversely, when we tested for `hasSufficientFunds`, we ensured that the transaction was being called by the owner. This way, the owner does not get in the way of what we are testing for.

Now, let's move on to a crucial aspect of writing smart contracts and testing them—**events**.

Testing for Solidity events

We briefly touched on testing for events but we did not get into much detail. Now is the time.

[138]

Events are a great way to let the client (frontend) know what has happened, and they're great for providing metadata about a transaction or public function invocation of your Solidity smart contract. Along with testing the state modifications of a transaction, return value of a `view` function, and modifiers, we can also test whether an event was emitted with the appropriate metadata.

Right now, our `TaskMaster` contract has no events. Let's quickly add one.

Inside the `TaskMaster.sol` file, underneath the state variable declarations and before the constructor, add the following line of code:

```
event LogRecipientRewarded(address recipient, uint rewardAmount);
```

This is how you declare an event in Solidity.

We call it `LogRecipientRewarded`. We also specify the metadata we want the event to contain; specifically, our event holds data about the recipient and reward amount.

Next, let's use this event. In other words, let's emit it from the `reward` function. Inside the `reward` function, after the accounting and before the `return` statement, add the following line of code:

```
LogRecipientRewarded(doer, rewardAmount);
```

We emit the event by calling it just like a function.

In it, we pass `doer` as the recipient and the `rewardAmount` as the reward amount. That's it—our `reward` function now emits this event.

Next, let's test that this event was indeed emitted!

Let's go back to the `test-task-master.js` test file and look inside the test for the `reward` function. Remember our `rewardTxObj` that was returned when the `Promise` of `reward` resolved?:

```
it('should be able to reward recipient', function() {
  const REWARD_WEI = 50;
  let originalOwnerBalance;
  let originalRecipientBalance;
  let instance;

  return TaskMaster.deployed()
    .then(_instance => {
      instance = _instance;
```

Testing Your Dapp

```
        return instance.getBalance.call(owner, { from: owner } );
    })
    .then(_originalOwnerBalance => {
      originalOwnerBalance = _originalOwnerBalance;
      return instance.getBalance.call(recipient, { from: owner } );
    })
    .then(_originalRecipientBalance => {
      originalRecipientBalance = _originalRecipientBalance;
      return instance.reward(recipient, REWARD_WEI, {
        from: owner
      });
    })
    .then(rewardTxObj => {
        return instance.getBalance.call(owner, { from: owner } );
    })
    .then(actualOwnerBalance => {
        assert.equal(actualOwnerBalance.toNumber(), +originalOwnerBalance - REWARD_WEI, `Owner should have ${REWARD_WEI} less`);
        return instance.getBalance.call(recipient, { from: owner } );
    })
    .then(actualRecipientBalance => {
        assert.equal(actualRecipientBalance.toNumber(), +originalRecipientBalance + REWARD_WEI, `Recipient should have ${REWARD_WEI} more`);
        return;
    });
});
```

Well, this is the same object that contains the event we've thrown!

Add `console.log` inside the `then` function to see what `rewardTransactionObject` looks like:

```
.then(rewardTxObj => {
    console.log(rewardTxObj);
    return instance.getBalance.call(owner, { from: owner } );
})
```

You should see the following output in your terminal console:

```
{ tx: '0xac95dd2d6bc719a30229f4c9a91a20389bb1fd424c781a0926fed9210111f8a3',
  receipt:
   { transactionHash:
'0xac95dd2d6bc719a30229f4c9a91a20389bb1fd424c781a0926fed9210111f8a3',
     transactionIndex: 0,
     blockHash:
'0xbc37fd5ebd1e4e6cca3efce9eb6a8f954d20e2b6b12b00054c10653ac90d0bf4',
     blockNumber: 18,
```

```
        gasUsed: 50748,
        cumulativeGasUsed: 50748,
        contractAddress: null,
        logs: [ [Object] ],
        status: 1 },
   logs:
    [ { logIndex: 0,
        transactionIndex: 0,
        transactionHash:
 '0xac95dd2d6bc719a30229f4c9a91a20389bb1fd424c781a0926fed9210111f8a3',
        blockHash:
 '0xbc37fd5ebd1e4e6cca3efce9eb6a8f954d20e2b6b12b00054c10653ac90d0bf4',
        blockNumber: 18,
        address: '0xdda6327139485221633a1fcd65f4ac932e60a2e1',
        type: 'mined',
        event: 'LogRecipientRewarded',
        args: [Object] } ] }
```

Look under the `logs` property of the transaction object and notice `event:
'LogRecipientRewarded'`.

As you can see, all events thrown so far are in the logs of the transaction object. So, let's assert that the `LogRecipientRewarded` event was thrown. Of course, we see that it has been, but let's write the code to test for this.

Before we call `instance.getBalance`, paste the following code to test that the event was thrown:

```
const LOG_RECIPIENT_REWARD = 'LogRecipientRewarded';
const recipientRewardedLog = rewardTxObj.logs[0];
assert.strictEqual(
  recipientRewardedLog.event,
  LOG_RECIPIENT_REWARD,
  `${LOG_RECIPIENT_REWARD} was not not thrown!`
);
```

We get the first element from the `logs` array, access the `event` property, and assert that it is indeed present.

Run your code. All of our tests should still be passing.

We still need to assert that the metadata of the event is what we expected. So, underneath the previous lines of code, add the following to test that the recipient and reward amount from the event logs match what we passed in:

```
const recipientFromLog = recipientRewardedLog.args.recipient;
```

Testing Your Dapp

```
const rewardAmountFromLog =
recipientRewardedLog.args.rewardAmount.toNumber();
assert.strictEqual(
  recipientFromLog,
  recipient,
  `Recipient should be ${recipient}`
);
assert.strictEqual(
  rewardAmountFromLog,
  REWARD_WEI,
  `Reward amount should be ${REWARD_WEI}`
);
```

We can get the event data by accessing the `args` property of `recipientRewardLog`. The `args` property contains information about the recipient and reward that was passed in when this event was emitted. Recall...:

```
LogRecipientRewarded(doer, rewardAmount);
```

Then, we assert as usual.

Run the tests again, and you should see them all pass. That's it!

The final test file should look like the one here: `https://github.com/PacktPublishing/Truffle-Quick-Start-Guide/blob/master/chapter6/test/test-task-master.js`.

Good job! Now you know how to access events from transaction objects and test for them.

If you find that your Solidity function is causing the EVM to throw a revert and you are unsure why, it could be that one of the modifiers or `assert/revert/require` statements are getting in the way.

But how do you know which one?

You can simply comment out all of the modifiers and `assert/revert/require` statements, and slowly comment them back in, one at a time. This way, you can isolate them and find the statement that is causing your transaction to revert.

Summary

We've covered a lot here! You learned how to write unit tests in Solidity and JavaScript. Specifically, you learned how to test for modifiers, public functions, state modifications, and events! Remember, testing is a vital part of any software development—not just smart contract development. Just as with any software, writing unit tests is absolutely crucial to ensuring that your application works well in production and makes users happy.

See you in `Chapter 7`, *Truffle Gotchas and Best Practices*, where we learn about best practices and gotchas in Truffle!

7
Truffle Gotchas and Best Practices

This chapter will teach you about the common mistakes people make when developing with Truffle, as well as how to remedy them. Moreover, you will learn how to apply best practices when developing your smart contract. Lastly, you will learn and understand how to diagnose and resolve common blockchain issues such as chain syncing, as well as some best security practices.

More specifically, you will:

- Learn and understand the differences between gas, gas price, and gas limit
- Learn and understand how to diagnose and resolve common blockchain issues such as chain syncing
- Learn and understand security practices

Gas versus gas limit versus gas price

One of the most common concepts to get your head around is the the difference between gas, gas price, and gas limit. Knowing the difference between these different things is crucial. Let's start with gas.

Gas

Every transaction you do costs gas. What's gas? Well, it's the *fuel* needed to execute a transaction, denominated in `Gwei`, which is usually equal to $1*10^{-9}$ ETH. Recall the smallest denomination of ETH, `wei`, which is $1*10^{-18}$ ETH, that denominates the amount you will be paying for the transaction.

As we've seen before, you can specify a gas amount in a transaction. We've done this before using web3. Recall that in `Chapter 6`, *Testing Your Dapp*, we had the following line:

```
instance.reward(recipient, REWARD_WEI, { from: recipient, gas: 3000000 })
```

As you can see, we specify a gas of `3000000`.

We can also specify gas in our `truffle.js` file, as we've seen in `Chapter 4`, *Migrating Your Dapp to Ethereum Blockchains*:

```
// Allows us to use ES6 in our migrations and tests.
require('babel-register')

module.exports = {
  networks: {
    development: {
      host: '127.0.0.1',
      port: 8545,
      network_id: '*' // Match any network id
    },
    ropsten: {
      network_id: 3,
      host: "127.0.0.1",
      port: 8545,
      gas: 4612388
    }
  }
}
```

Chapter 7

As we covered in that chapter, the minimum gas amount for a transaction is `21000`. This means that in order to execute any transaction that needs to be mined by miners, you will need to supply a gas of at least `21000`.

Where does this go? Well, it goes to miner rewards. Miners spend their time and computing power verifying your transaction and, for that, they need some reward for it; that reward is the gas you pay.

If you execute a transaction but don't specify enough gas, you may get the following error in your console:

```
Intrinsic gas too low
```

Simply increase the gas for your transaction.

Similarly, if you're performing a transaction on an Ethereum network such as Ropsten or even the mainnet, the error will be specifed as such:

TxHash:	0x617248f5eb178f81a4aea5c986a0b858b137bfae777979723c5507a6491340fb
Block Height:	3844796 (117 block confirmations)
TimeStamp:	33 mins ago (Jun-09-2017 11:06:34 AM +UTC)
From:	0xe7a3aa2509ec62386debd90f65a7d4f19199dc38
To:	Contract 0xf92f7c8012de01ae247a2523e6e3a086273ab03a Warning! Error encountered during contract execution [Out of gas]
Value:	1.71 Ether ($451.27) - [CANCELLED]
Gas Limit:	59268
Gas Price:	0.000000020229599175 Ether
Gas Used By Txn:	59268
Actual Tx Cost/Fee:	0.0011989678839 Ether ($0.32)

Note the **Out of gas** message.

 The bottom line is, always be aware of gas costs when you perform a transaction.

Now, let's move on to gas price.

[147]

Gas price

Another term you will come across, and an option that you can specify, is gas price.

When performing a transaction, you can optionally set a gas price. Why? Well, it is the amount of `Gwei` you are willing to pay per unit of gas. So, you can offer a higher price, meaning your transaction will be mined faster. Why? Well, a higher gas price means a higher reward for the miner, giving the miner more incentive to mine the block with your transaction. So, you can *skip the queue* by offering to pay a high gas price.

It's fundamental economics. Miners want to maximize their profits so they look to accept the highest gas price, but that should still be low enough for them to be able to mine a sufficient number of transactions. Initiators of the transactions want to minimize their costs so they look to offer the lowest gas price possible, but that should still be high enough to have their transactions mined.

It's basic economics.

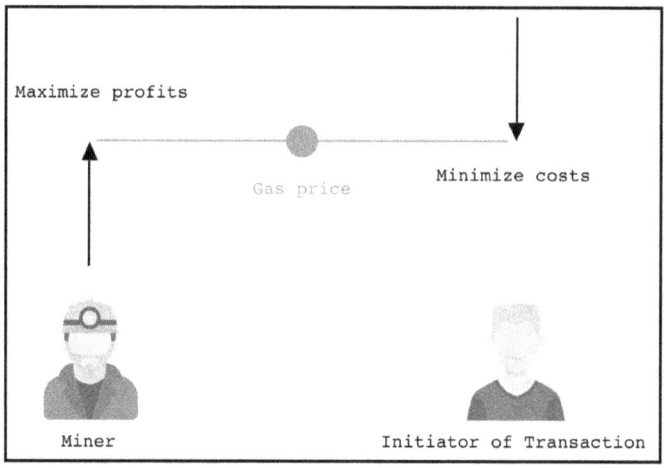

You can specify a gas price in your `truffle.js`:

```
// Allows us to use ES6 in our migrations and tests.
require('babel-register')

module.exports = {
  networks: {
    development: {
      host: '127.0.0.1',
      port: 8545,
```

```
      network_id: '*' // Match any network id
    },
    ropsten: {
      network_id: 3,
      host: "127.0.0.1",
      port: 8545,
      gas: 4612388,
      gasPrice: 20
    }
  }
}
```

The gas price is denominated in `Gwei`. Here, I've specified a gas price of 20 `Gwei`.

You can find the current gas prices that miners are willing to accept here: https://ethgasstation.info/. Currently, the standard gas price being accepted by miners is 6 `Gwei`:

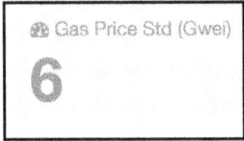

You can also see the recommended gas prices depending on how fast you want your transaction to be processed and mined. Again, these numbers vary quite often.

Speed	Gas Price (gwei)
SafeLow (<30m)	6
Standard (<5m)	6
Fast (<2m)	9

Recommended Gas Prices (based on current network conditions)

 If you want your transaction to be mined relatively quickly, increase the gas price.

Truffle Gotchas and Best Practices

Let's move on to gas limit.

Gas limit

Gas is not always deterministic, and as a sender of a transaction, you want to protect yourself against spending too much gas. For example, suppose you are looping through an array of unknown size. Firstly, unbounded looping is an anti-pattern. Why? Well, as the sender of the transaction, you have no way of predicting the gas that will be incurred by the loop. If the array has only one element, that's fine. But, suppose the array has multiple elements, say 1,000, or 10,000? The gas costs will be tremendously high.

Or, suppose you accidentally have an infinite loop that you are unaware of. Again, your gas costs will be very high if you don't set a limit and allow your transaction to be mined and processed.

So, to protect yourself, you can set a gas limit—the maximum gas you are willing pay for the transaction.

You can do so in your `truffle.js` file:

```
// Allows us to use ES6 in our migrations and tests.
require('babel-register')

module.exports = {
  networks: {
    development: {
      host: '127.0.0.1',
      port: 8545,
      network_id: '*' // Match any network id
    },
    ropsten: {
      network_id: 3,
      host: "127.0.0.1",
      port: 8545,
      gas: 4612388,
      gasLimit:5000000
    }
  }
}
```

Here, we set a gas limit of `500000`.

Great, now let's see how we can handle the very common sync issues you may encounter when using Geth.

Sync issues in Geth

When you attempt to sync to Geth, you will notice that quite often, Geth simply takes too long to sync. To combat this, many developers turn to Parity. It is simply a faster sync.

Another common mistake you will make is knowing for a fact that your account has a positive balance, but when you go to check the balance, you see that it has zero balance.

The reason for this is that you are probably not synced.

To ensure you are synced, while a Geth or Parity node is running, you can run the following code inside a JavaScript console:

```
web3.eth.syncing
```

You may see a JavaScript object returned, such as this:

```
{
    currentBlock: 236124,
    highestBlock: 2947915,
    knownStates: 1320304,
    pulledStates: 1320304,
    startingBlock: 236111
}
```

If you see this, it means you are still currently syncing on your Ethereum client. You can see the highest block, which is `2947915`, and the current block, which is `236124`. The current block is much, much less than the highest block, meaning we still have a way to go before we finish our sync. This is not uncommon when using Geth. Luckily, you have plenty of fast sync options, as we covered in previous chapters when using Parity.

So, how do we know that our client is fully synced? Well, when you run `web3.eth.syncing`, you may see this:

```
false
```

This means that your client is fully synced!

Great, let's move on to security best practices.

Security best practices

As you may recall, in previous chapters, we created a `password.txt` file in the root level of our project containing the password to unlock our coinbase account. This was stored in plain text. Of course, this is not the best way to store your passwords: out in the open, in plain text.

How do we make it more secure?

You can put the `password.txt` file in your `.gitignore` file. This way, it won't be tracked by Git's version control.

For all other sensitive phrases, passwords or keys, it is also best to store a hard copy of them. In other words, store them offline. Why? This way, your sensitive data is not vulnerable to hackers. If it is offline, only you have it. So, a good idea is to store your passwords on a sheet of paper.

Of course, the next big question is, what if you lose that sheet of paper? It is a single point of failure. Well, the answer to that is... don't have a single point of failure! Store a few copies, in separate places.

Summary

Congratulations! You have learned not only the best practices and gotchas in Truffle, but how to build secure, robust, and scalable decentralized applications. This was no easy task, and you've covered a lot throughout this book. You are now ready to build real-world, decentralized applications, join a blockchain company as an engineer, build your own ICO, or do whatever you choose to do.

Thanks for working through this book. Take care until next time.

Other Books You May Enjoy

If you enjoyed this book, you may be interested in these other books by Packt:

Mastering Blockchain – Second Edition
Imran Bashir

ISBN: 978-1-78883-904-4

- Master the theoretical and technical foundations of the blockchain technology
- Understand the concept of decentralization, its impact, and its relationship with blockchain technology
- Master how cryptography is used to secure data - with practical examples
- Grasp the inner workings of blockchain and the mechanisms behind bitcoin and alternative cryptocurrencies
- Understand the theoretical foundations of smart contracts
- Learn how Ethereum blockchain works and how to develop decentralized applications using Solidity and relevant development frameworks
- Identify and examine applications of the blockchain technology - beyond currencies
- Investigate alternative blockchain solutions including Hyperledger, Corda, and many more
- Explore research topics and the future scope of blockchain technology

Other Books You May Enjoy

Ethereum Smart Contract Development
Mayukh Mukhopadhyay

ISBN: 978-1-78847-304-0

- Know how to build your own smart contracts and cryptocurrencies
- Understand the Solidity language
- Find out about data types, control structure, functions, inheritance, mathematical operations, and much more
- See the various types of forks and discover how they are related to Ethereum
- Get to know the various concepts of web3.js and its APIs so you can build client-side apps
- Build a DAO from scratch and acquire basic knowledge of DApps on Ethercast
- Be guided through the project so you can optimize EVM for smart contracts
- Build your own decentralized applications (DApps) by taking a practical approach

Leave a review - let other readers know what you think

Please share your thoughts on this book with others by leaving a review on the site that you bought it from. If you purchased the book from Amazon, please leave us an honest review on this book's Amazon page. This is vital so that other potential readers can see and use your unbiased opinion to make purchasing decisions, we can understand what our customers think about our products, and our authors can see your feedback on the title that they have worked with Packt to create. It will only take a few minutes of your time, but is valuable to other potential customers, our authors, and Packt. Thank you!

Index

A

angular-truffle-starter-dapp
  about 89
  src folder 90
Angular
  reference, for tutorial 88
application migration
  about 70, 71
  contract, migrating to Kovan 83, 84
  contract, migrating to Ropsten 81, 82
  contracts, migrating to Ropsten with Parity 71, 72, 74, 75
  funds, adding to Parity coinbase account 78, 79
  Parity, syncing to Ropsten 77, 78
  pitfalls 84, 85
  Ropsten Parity account, creating 75, 76
arrays 40

D

Dapp
  build steps, performing 20, 21, 22, 24
  building 9, 88
  contract, securing with modifiers 17, 18
  folders, viewing 13
  JavaScript, writing 24, 25, 26, 27, 28, 29, 30
  owner, adding 15
  reward method, creating 16
  root files, viewing 13
  smart contract, writing 14
  styling 20
  TaskMaster.sol file, creating 18, 19
  to-do list, building 9, 10, 11
  Truffle project, initializing 11, 12
  unnecessary files and folders, deleting 14
  user interface, building 19
  utility method, adding 18

data types, Solidity
  about 40
  arrays 40
  mapping 41
  structs 40
dependency injection, Angular
  reference 94

E

Ethereum client
  about 50, 51
  Ganache-CLI 59
  Geth 51
  Parity 55
  reference 63
  selecting 63
  with Truffle 63
Ethereum Stack Exchange
  reference 85
Ethereum subreddit
  reference 85
events, Solidity 46
EVM (Ethereum virtual machine) 24

F

faucet
  about 79
  reference 79
folders, Dapp
  app 13
  contracts 13
  migrations 13
  tests 13
function modifiers, Solidity 44, 45
function types, Solidity
  pure 46

reference 46
view 45
functions, Solidity
  about 42
  external visibility specifier 42
  internal visibility specifier 42
  private visibility specifier 42
  public visibility specifier 42
  reference 42, 43

G

Ganache-CLI
  about 33, 36, 37, 50, 59
  actions 61, 62
  features 59, 60
  installing 33
  Truffle, integrating 66
gas 146
gas limit 150
gas price 148, 149
Geth
  about 50, 51
  actions 54, 55
  features 52, 53
  functions 51
  reference 51, 52
  sync issues 151
  Truffle, integrating 64, 65

J

JavaScript
  unit tests, writing 127, 128, 130, 131, 134, 135, 136, 137

K

Kovan
  contract, migrating 83, 84

M

mapping 41
MetaCoinService 98, 99, 100, 103
MetaMask
  about 79
  reference 79

mining, Geth
  reference 55

N

network ID
  reference 54
NgZone
  reference 95

P

Parity
  about 50, 55
  actions 57, 58
  contracts, migrating to Ropsten 71, 72, 74, 75
  features 55
  funds, adding to coinbase account 78, 79
  reference 55, 78
  Ropsten Parity account, creating 75, 76
  syncing, to Ropsten 77, 78
  Truffle, integrating 65, 66
  using 56, 57

R

root files, Dapp
  package.json 13
  truffle.js 13
Ropsten
  about 71
  contract, migrating 81, 82
  contracts, migrating with Parity 71, 72, 74, 75
  Parity, syncing 77, 78
  Ropsten Parity account, creating 75, 76

S

security
  best practices 152
Solidity events
  testing for 139, 140, 142
Solidity unit tests
  reference 126
Solidity
  about 39
  data types 40
  events 46

function modifiers 44, 45
function types 45
functions 42, 43
  reference 39
  unit tests, writing 118, 119
  visibility specifiers 41
special variables
  reference 43
starter Dapp
  running 91, 93, 94, 95
structs 40
sync issues, Geth 151

T

Tachyons CSS library
  reference 20
  using 20
TaskMaster
  testing 120, 121, 122, 123, 125, 126
to-do list
  building 9, 10, 11
TodoCoin 16
transaction object
  reference 130
Truffle, and React code
  exploring 102, 104
Truffle, and React starter
  reference 100
truffle-react folder structure
  about 101
  src folder 102

Truffle
  about 8, 9
  and Angular 88
  and Node 106
  and React 100
  integrating, with Ganache-CLI 66
  integrating, with Geth 64, 65
  integrating, with Parity 65, 66
  Node Run Steps 107, 108, 111, 113
  Web3 37, 39
  with Ethereum clients 63

U

unit tests
  writing, with JavaScript 127, 128, 130, 131, 134, 135, 136, 137
  writing, with Solidity 118, 119

V

visibility specifiers, Solidity
  about 41
  internal 41
  private 41
  public 41

W

Web3
  about 32, 33
  Ganache-CLI 33, 34, 36, 37
  in Truffle 37, 39
Web3Service 96, 97

[159]

www.ingramcontent.com/pod-product-compliance
Lightning Source LLC
Chambersburg PA
CBHW082248220526
45469CB00009B/2913